# GAMES FOR TRAINERS
## Volume 2

# Games for Trainers
## Volume 2

ANDY KIRBY

Gower

Published by
Gower Publishing Company Limited
Gower House
Croft Road
Aldershot
Hants GU11 3HR
England

**British Library Cataloguing in Publication Data**
Kirby, Andy
  Games for trainers. Vol.2
  I. Title
  371.397

  Reprinted 1993

  ISBN 0–566–07290–4

Phototypeset by Intype, London
Printed in England by Clays Ltd, St Ives plc

# Contents

# Preface

This book is a companion volume to *Games for Trainers Volume 1*, and I wrote it for much the same reason; a wish to share my own enthusiasm for and experience of training games. That volume analysed the role of training games, and discussed some important considerations in using them. In this volume I offer a further 75 games.

As in the earlier volume, the games are presented in a standard for mat which sets out the Title, Summary, Objectives, Materials Needed, Timing, Procedure, Commentary (on using the game in practice) and Variations. This is followed by an Index of Games by Objectives. Many of the games can be used to achieve more than one objective; this index will enable you to locate all the activities which might be used to explore a particular teaching point. Of course, some uses for particular games will occur to you that I haven't even considered.

As in the earlier volume, some of the 75 games described in this volume will be old friends under new names, and I make no claim to have invented the majority of them from scratch. I have tried to tap that collective trainers' unconscious from which so many of our ideas and activities emerge, and to which we return them in an enriched form. What I have done is to codify a variety of the training games that I use, with some suggestions as to ways of using them to meet a variety of training needs. Even if you are familiar with the activity itself, however, you may find the way in which the structure has been described, some of the variations, or the training objectives worth reading. I would welcome correspondence from readers about variations they have tried to these games, thoughts they may have on the formulation of the games, and any new games they may wish to propose for inclusion in possible future editions. All such contributions will be acknowledged.

Andy Kirby

# Acknowledgements

I acknowledge the help of all the delegates and trainers who have encouraged me to devise, develop, improve and, on occasions, abandon games. Colleagues and former colleagues at Environment Training Services, the Birkbeck College Centre for Extra-Mural Studies, the Mary Ward Centre and Roffey Park Management College have all contributed to my interest in and enthusiasm for games. I would particularly like to thank CarolAnn Ashton, Paula Bullock, Lucy Britton, Sue Dean, Alan Margolis and Clare Shaw. Sarah Boland's advice on an earlier version of the manuscript has been invaluable. Many of the games described in this book have origins unknown to me, and I offer my thanks to the unknown inventors of those activities. Malcolm Stern's editorial advice has made the preparation of my first book for publication considerably less painful and more productive than it might have otherwise been. Finally, I would like to acknowledge the patience of my lover Mick Harrison for suffering my preoccupation with this project over the past eighteen months.

AK

# 1
# The objectives used in this book

The activities in this book are indexed by the nature of their learning objective (see pp. 155–63). The specific objectives of each session will have to be formulated by the trainer, if appropriate, in the usual "by the end of the session participants will be able to . . ." formula. I have used the following definitions:

- *Action planning* – an essential part of any course will be the element of action planning in which participants seek to apply what they have learned to their work.
- *Assertiveness* – the distinction between assertive, aggressive and passive behaviour patterns is frequently made in social and life skills training. For a history of the concept of assertiveness see Rakos (1986).
- *Attention switching* – activities with a high reflective content can leave participants thinking too hard and long about the issues raised for them when there are other matters to be covered on the course. One way of overcoming this is through a quick attention switching exercise. Most of them are also energizers, but are here being used for a slightly different purpose.
- *Attributions* – courses on equal opportunities frequently explore the question of attributions – the assumptions that can be made about people belonging to a particular group or category. In this connection I also include attributions made of other course members or about other people in a working group – which may be explored in a team-building course.
- *Counselling* – in addition to the listening skills objective below, there are some abilities particularly demanded of personal counsellors.
- *Creativity* – this refers to the development of the ability to find

new ideas and concepts rather than the solving of practical problems, though the same exercises may often be used for both purposes.

- *Decision making* – most of these activities concern the process of decision making in groups.
- *Energizer* – at certain times on a course (the "pudding session" first thing after lunch is a classic instance), participants will lack energy and concentration. An energizer is an activity with no other purpose than to get the blood flowing and to re-establish a group after a break, usually through physical activity. They should be used enthusiastically but carefully, since delegates with a cynical approach to participative training tend to react particularly negatively to these apparently purposeless activities. I keep a few energizers in reserve, and allow any member of the group to ask for an energizer. If the feeling of the group is that one is needed then it can be brought in. I would not recommend using the same energizer twice on a course.
- *Expectations* – it is often useful in a course to establish the expectations that group members have brought with them.
- *Feedback* – the principles of feedback may well be covered before a game begins if participants have to give feedback to one another. They can usefully form part of a group contract (see Vol. 1, pp. 16–18). Feedback will often be an objective in its own right (for example, in appraisal interviewing training), and the principles can form the basis of the input part of such a session.
- *Introductions* – a repertoire of introduction exercises is useful. If you are part of a training community it is a good idea to allocate these to specific courses. Energizers can help to break the tension during the introductory phase of the group life. Used at this point, they are often referred to as "icebreakers".
- *Leadership* – one aspect of team-building is the operation of group leaders. The activities listed under this title can be adapted to bring out this particular learning point.
- *Listening skills* – a wide variety of active listening skills and non-verbal sensitivities can be taught through the use of games. They are of use in a whole range of courses covering personal effectiveness, workplace skills, counselling and customer care.
- *Motivation* – the objective of asking participants to question their own motivation can be important in allowing them to consider alternative courses of action (for example, on culture change programmes). It can also form part of management training where delegates are trying to improve their own understanding of the principles of human motivation.
- *Negotiation* – where groups have shared resources then negotiation must take place to ensure that the needs of all those

involved are met. Most leadership courses will require this objective to be included.

- *Non-verbal communication* – most of the games in this book can be used to heighten sensitivity to non-verbal signals. With the games indicated this is particularly the case, and they might be useful on courses with customer care or face-to-face communication themes.
- *Presentational skills* – some games have an element of self-presentation, either before all or part of the group. The games listed under this title are the ones where this is important in its own right, where feedback can be offered.
- *Problem solving* – the distinction between problem solving and creativity has been described above. The emphasis here is on the solving of practical problems using all of the resources available in an effective and efficient manner.
- *Self-disclosure* – this can sometimes be useful in its own right to establish a culture of frankness and trust, but it is also an important part of self-development and team-building courses. During self disclosure games it is often useful to remind the group of the confidentiality terms of their contract.
- *Self-perception* – an increase in understanding of how one is, and the relationship between that and the way that one is perceived by other people.
- *Stress management* – the management of stress has recently become a growth area for trainers. Most of the exercises with this objective involve some form of physical or mental relaxation.
- *Team-building* – many objectives centre on encouraging teams to be more effective at working together. Most of the games in this book can be steered in this direction through correct processing, but for some it is important enough to have a specific objective.
- *Trainer training* – it is possible to use any of the games in this book for trainer training, but there are some which are especially well suited to this purpose and they have been indicated by reference to this objective.
- *Trust* – to impart an understanding of the preconditions necessary to trust someone, and the degree to which that trust is extended.
- *Validation* – these exercises will assess the learning of some particular skill or knowledge covered elsewhere on a course, or help ascertain the impressions of a group of participants of a course or any of its activities. (This must be differentiated from the evaluation of the worth of the objectives of the course to the client.)
- *Verbal/written communication* – these core areas of training need no explanation.

# 2

# The games

A Gender Setting
All About Me
Amorous Andy
Antimastermind
Archaeological Digs
Babel
Battle of the Sexes
Blind Walk
Bunker
Can I Come to the Party?
Chains of Command
Chain Whispers
Chorus Line
Class of their Own
Confessions of a Trombone
  Welder
Continuum
Creatriptych
Creativity Quotient
Cutting Rose's Hair
Discriminet
Domination
Do You Come Here Often?
Dracula has Risen from the
  Grave
Flattery
Fleet Street Fog
Fruit Salad
The Game Game
General Assembly
Go-Go
Goodies

Gripes Auction
Grouptalk
Helping Hands
If Eggs Could Fly
If I Were You
In the Neck
It's Not Fair!
Knots
Learnabout
Legover
Lemon and Lime
Little Attentions
Lost for Words
The Missing Link
Mommie Said . . .
Naked City
Obits
Odd Objects
One-A
On the Other Hand
Packtivity
Picture Hunt
Pillow Talk
Poetry in Motion
Remote
Research Rap
Resents and Appreciates
Right Pickle
Sharks
Shiatsu Shuffle
Sixty-second Solos
Speaking Statues

5

# A Gender Setting

**Summary**    Participants have to guess the gender of a member.

**Objectives**   Verbal communication.
Equal opportunities.
Team-building.

**Materials**    Pens and paper.

**Timing**   30 minutes.

**Procedure**   1.  Form the group into two teams with men and women in each team. Ask one team to choose a group member as the subject, without the other group knowing who the subject is.
2.  The task of the second team is to ascertain if the subject is male or female. They can ask any question they like but must ask it of the whole of the other team which can then confer the answer.
3.  Explain to the answering team that they may lie and may refuse to answer a question if they wish.
4.  The first team may guess at the gender of the subject once only, but can ask as many questions as they like before they do so.
5.  Discuss how the group reached its decision, whether there is any unequivocal way of making such a determination, what implications this has for equal opportunities, the way the group worked as a team, or whatever is the learning point of the game.

**Commentary**  This activity requires a mixed sex group. In this case it is necessary for the trainer to be involved in dividing the group so that there are some of each sex in each group. This division, however, should not lead to an excessively competitive attitude between the teams. This activity is based on a thought experiment suggested by Alan Turing (1950).

**Variations**   1.  This game can also be played on the basis of distinctions of

7

sexual orientation, social class, race or any classification that can be used to divide people into two categories.

2. It can also be played in pairs or triads (one being an observer feeding into a discussion session) using one of these distinctions with the trainer "floating" between pairs.

# All About Me

**Summary**    Participants make a series of self-disclosures to other single group members in quick succession.

**Objectives**    Self-disclosure.
Team-building.

**Materials**    None.

**Timing**    30 minutes.

**Procedure**
1. Ask participants to form pairs and to take turns in talking about themselves for two minutes. The listener may indicate interest non-verbally, but must say nothing.
2. Repeat with a new partner.
3. Repeat a third time allowing five minutes.
4. Repeat again twice.
5. With the last partner explore any changes in the kinds of things that were mentioned. Deal with any other feedback in the main group but do not force disclosure of what was discussed in the pairs.

**Commentary**    This activity requires a degree of trust within the group, and is best not done too early in the group's life. It tends to divert people away from making a "standard" self-disclosure. The trainer will have to take part to make a pair if necessary.

**Variation**    On a team-building course the material disclosed can relate more to the participants' team roles.

# Amorous Andy

**Summary**    An introductions exercise in which participants introduce themselves with a word starting with the first letter of their given name.

**Objectives**    Introductions.

**Materials**    None.

**Timing**    Five minutes.

**Procedure**

1. Form the participants into a circle and say that you are going to suggest a brief exercise which will help people to learn each other's names.
2. Ask each person to introduce themselves by a word beginning with the same letter or initial sound as their name. Give an example using your own name, and one for someone else (for example, "I'm Andy and I'm amusing"). The word doesn't have to be true.
3. Invite someone to start.

**Commentary**    This is a good exercise for the start of a second day, and a good one if a new person or guest speaker joins a ready-formed group. The words act as useful "pegs" for memory, and ensures the new person becomes involved to the same level as the others really quickly. If the exercise needs a name I suggest the trainer name the exercise after him or herself as I have done.

**Variations**

1. Use words that rhyme with the person's name ("I'm Andy and I'm feeling randy"). This does not always work if there are a number of ethnic minority participants whose names might not rhyme with many English words.
2. Relate the words chosen to a picnic or a party ("I'm Andy and I'll bring anchovies", or "I'm Andy and I'll bring the brandy" in the rhyming version).

10

# Antimastermind

**Summary**     A circle-centre energizer in which the person at the centre must not mention a certain subject.

**Objectives**   Energizer.
Attention switching
Verbal communication.

**Materials**    Chairs, and if possible one chair like the BBC's *Mastermind*.
Prepared subject cards.

**Timing**       Ten minutes.

**Procedure**    1.  Remind participants of the principles of the British quiz show *Mastermind* – that the contestant has to answer questions on their specialist subject as quickly as possible for two minutes. Introduce **Antimastermind**, in which the person in the chair has to *avoid* mentioning the specialist subject. The principles are that the person in the centre should (i) try to give the right answer, (ii) not mention the subject on the card, and (iii) should not repeat him or her self. For example, if the subject was "forks" then your answer to the question "What do you use to eat peas with" might be "An item of cutlery", but this would mean that you could not use the word "cutlery" again.
2.  Put yourself in the centre, take a subject and invite participants to frame questions to put to you. Questions do not have to be asked in any order – it is a free-for-all. The person asking the question that catches you out becomes "it", and has to take your place in the centre.
3.  Run through a few rounds with a new topic for each person in the centre, and allow a few moments for the framing of the questions.

**Commentary** Specialist subjects might be "soil", "tea", "computers" and "sex".

**Variation**    A longer version of the game could follow the format of *Mastermind* more accurately, with the naming of the contestant, applause, naming of the specialist subject, "I've started so I'll finish", etc.

# Archaeological Digs

**Summary**      Discovery exercise with a given object.

**Objectives**    Creativity.
                Attributions.

**Materials**     Pens and paper.
                Separate rooms for each group.
                A variety of small objects – (for example, fruits, sachet of sugar
                substitute, ice cube tray, teabag, corn, button, plastic connector from
                the top of four drinks cans, compact disc, Rubik's cube, thermos
                flask, candle, fuse, bicycle pump nozzle, can opener, glass ashtray,
                paper clip, spark plug, thimble, small musical instruments, items of
                cosmetics, kitchen implements, etc.).

**Timing**       30 minutes.

**Procedure**    1.  Explain that archaeologists sometimes find objects on digs and
                    do not know what they are. They have to use their imagin-
                    ations. They are to imagine that they are archaeologists 1000
                    years hence, and have discovered an object. They are to think
                    of as many *different* ideas as they can as to what each object is
                    used for.
                2.  Ask participants to form groups, hand out wrapped objects and
                    send groups into separate rooms.
                3.  Ask them to come back and report their findings to an archaeol-
                    ogical convention. The other groups can challenge the uses of
                    the object.

**Variations**   1.  Keep the instructions to "take this object away and find out as
                    much as you can about it." In that case there will be many
                    process points to discuss.
                2.  Invite the other groups to guess what the object is in the light
                    of the uses mentioned.
                3.  Instead of guessing uses, ask the other groups to make infer-
                    ences about twentieth century culture on the basis of the object.

Some objects will be richer than others for this purpose, and ones with visual representations will be best.

# Babel

**Summary**      Building exercise as individuals, and in groups.

**Objectives**   Team-building.
Objective setting.
Assertiveness.

**Materials**    Pens and paper.
Building materials (such as sugar cubes, old paper cups, tin cans, dominoes, old playing cards, or lego bricks).

**Timing**       45 minutes.

**Procedure**    1.  Ask individuals to estimate the height of the tower that they can build with the materials available in five minutes. The tower must be on the floor and be capable of supporting itself for 30 seconds. Ask them to write down their answer, but to keep it to themselves.
2.  Give them five minutes to build the tower and write down its height.
3.  Discuss as a group whether people overestimated or underestimated what they could do, and why this might have been the case. Consider whether issues other than height (such as structural stability, aesthetics) came into play.

**Commentary**   The lego version of this task is a management training classic, which can be refined by charging groups for resources (including time) on a sliding scale, allocating payment to different heights of tower, economy in use of bricks, etc.

**Variations**   1.  If the objective is team-building then after Stage 2 ask the members to form groups of three or four and carry out the game again. You may require public estimates from people or groups, in which case you will need a whiteboard or flipchart. Explore group working and the role of competition. Conclude with the building of one tower if you wish.

2. Have people working in pairs.
3. Change the task to making a paper plane and estimating how far it will fly, or to how long a chain of paper clips it is possible to make (the limit is the weight the top clip can support).
4. Form syndicates which work on the tasks with supervisors, who are the only ones to be briefed. Then add a further constraint to the task (like having constructors blindfolded, constructors are only to use their non-dominant hand).

# Battle of the Sexes

**Summary**      Examination of attributions about men and women.

**Objectives**   Attributions.
                 Team-building.

**Materials**    Prepared newsprint.
                 Pens.
                 Blank newsprint.

**Timing**       45 minutes.

**Procedure**    1. Divide participants into two teams of men and women and give
                    them a prepared newsprint. For the men headed "Because I
                    am a man I must . . .", and for the women "Because I am a
                    woman I must . . .". Ask them to go into separate rooms and
                    generate as many ideas as they can for ways to finish the
                    sentence. Allow them ten minutes in which to do this.
                 2. At the end of the period go into the rooms with a second sheet
                    and give them a further ten minutes. The sheets will be, for
                    the men, "If I were a woman I could . . .", and for the women
                    "If I were a man I could . . .".
                 3. Still in their groups, exchange the sheets. Ask them to discuss
                    what they have been given and think of questions of clarifi-
                    cation for the other group.
                 4. After ten minutes unite the group, asking participants *not* to sit
                    as separate groups. Discuss the extent to which men and
                    women have to be what they say they do, and to what extent
                    they can have the qualities that they have given to the opposite
                    sex.
                 5. Ask participants to form pairs and share what they have learned
                    about themselves from the exercise.

**Commentary** At least three people from each sex are necessary for this to be a
               viable game. Also, consider your ability to process what might come
               out of this exercise. One of my male group participants produced

17

"If I were a woman I could get away with anything I wanted once a month"!

**Variation**   Use other categories into which the group can be divided. In team-building this might be managers and staff or corporate and divisional.

# Blind Walk

**Summary**      Participants take it in turn to be led sightless by a partner.

**Objectives**   Trust.
Attention switching.

**Materials**    As many as possible.

**Timing**       30 minutes.

**Procedure**    1.  Ask subjects to form pairs in which each person is an A or a B.
2.  A is to lead B on a blind walk. A should guide from behind with a hand on B's shoulder and the other hand on B's wrist. A should adopt the pace of B, and guide only where necessary or where they want to expose B to something different. A should not allow B to leave the room. B's should become receptive to their senses, and should not try to work out where in the room they are. Guides should start by gently rotating their subjects a few times.
3.  The trainer should say that s/he will be "varying the experience" and can use water, pencil sharpeners, perfumes or anything to hand to involve the senses of the subjects. In a trusting group where there is no anxiety abut bodily contact, the subjects can be brought together in a circle. After a while subjects open their eyes and the roles are reversed.

**Commentary**   This exercise can easily last ten minutes each way. An attention switching exercise is usually needed afterwards.

**Variation**    If the grounds of the training venue permit, this activity can take place outdoors.

# Bunker

**Summary**      Decision making survival task.

**Objectives**      Team-building.
Attributions.
Assertiveness.

**Materials**      Prepared sheets (see below).
Pens and paper.

**Timing**      One hour.

**Procedure**

1. Hand out the instruction sheet to the participants and give them 30 minutes in which to reach their decision. A large group can be divided into two. Impress the emergency on the groups by counting them down. Clarify the instructions if necessary, but do not add to the information given.
2. Discuss as a group the basis on which the decision was reached. You can put some input into the group processes that you have been observing.

**Commentary**   You may need to vary the material to meet the needs of a group (the disabilities should not reflect those of any group members if this can be avoided). Group members sometimes criticise this exercise as being unrealistic in that decisions are being taken on insufficient evidence. Point out that this is often the case in real life, though. Some facts about the group have been carefully balanced (gender, child-bearing status), and others have been left deliberately vague for most cases (like religion). You may find that group members develop assumptions as to what these are.

**Variations**

1. Allocate the roles of the potential survivors to members of the group and ask them to defend their case for survival. This is called the *Balloon Game* because a common version has three people in a sinking balloon arguing why they should not be thrown out.

2.  Other scenarios for the decision to be made are:

    (a)  a kidney dialysis machine with the capacity to take five more patients;
    (b)  a nuclear war where the bunker has only limited capacity;
    (c)  a spacecraft leaving the doomed earth with a limited number of spaces;
    (d)  the rescue of underground volunteers in an experiment on living in confined spaces where you are only able to rescue them one at a time to a timescale which means that those left until last are likely to drown;
    (e)  or any other scenario where life and death decisions affecting others cannot be avoided.

3.  You can allow some of the participants to have relationships (family, sexual, emotional, professional) with others, which adds another an element of interdependency to the choices.

# Bunker – Instruction sheet

In 40 minutes a passing comet will destroy all human life on earth, which will enter a period of cold and darkness for three months. Scientists believe the earth will be incapable of supporting human life. You are safe. You are in a bunker which will support you in cramped but tolerable conditions for six months, after which you can venture out. To your knowledge you are the only people in the world who will survive. The bunker is capable of supporting a further five people only, and the doors will not close until all the places are filled. There are ten people outside from whom you have to choose the other survivors. They are as follows:

**Tamra – Biologist** – Brazilian, female, 31, world expert in the ecology of rain forests and the possible effects of nuclear winter. During field work has developed skills in animal husbandry. Wheelchair bound as a result of a helicopter crash on a field trip.

**Kenda – Student** – black, male, 23, studying for a PhD in metallurgy. Good general education ending up at Imperial College, London University. Has been studying for six years and has an extension on the completion of his degree. His supervisor has doubts whether he will actually complete it.

**Paul – Farm worker** – white, male, 59, widowed rheumatic and with impaired hearing. Wide experience and good knowledge of all aspects of farming.

**Lu – Mechanical engineer** – Chinese, female, 34, was doing a check-up on the ventilation system in the bunker when the emergency began. Wide knowledge of microprocessor operated control systems.

**Rick – Dentist** – male, Australian, 25, fit. Positive for HIV (the virus that causes AIDS).

**Maureen – Cook** – female, white 46, divorced and working in a nearby canteen. Has a wide experience of catering. Following her divorce and a series of unsuccessful relationships has developed a drink problem.

**Gorda – Child** – Malaysian, male, eight years old. Fat, spoiled by his doting parents, intelligent and a little precocious. Teachers and educational psychologists predict a good future for him academically.

**Len – Security guard** – black, male, 29, dishonourably discharged from the army after the discovery of sexual relationships with other soldiers following front-line experience in the Falklands conflict for which he was decorated. Carries a pistol.

**Marek – Counsellor** – Polish, male, 57. Has worked in psychology, speech therapy. Well regarded in his profession. Blind.

**Farna – Doctor** – Pakistani, female, 31, works at a clinic for sexually transmitted diseases. Although liberal in her views on the role of women she intends her children to receive a Muslim upbringing.

**Alice – Teacher** – white, female, 27, has worked with children from all ages, recently recovered from a drug overdose and is still taking anti-depressants.

# Can I Come to the Party?

**Summary**      Deductions based on non-verbal cues.

**Objective**    Energizer.
Attention switching.
Non-verbal communication.

**Materials**    None.

**Timing**       Ten minutes plus.

**Procedure**    1.  Sit participants in a circle and explain that you are going to hold a party to which they may or may not be able to come. Invite them to ask if they can come to the party and say what they will wear. The person who guesses on what basis you are allowing people to come then takes over the game.

2.  Answer them according to some criterion which you have previously established. For example you may invite:

    those whose chosen clothing ends with a consonant;
    those who have their feet crossed when they ask to be invited;
    those who ask to be invited when you have your feet crossed;
    those who ask to be invited using your first name.

3.  If participants are not guessing then offer a hint (for instance, for the first example "No Lucy, you can't come wearing a bra, but you could come if you were wearing suspenders".

4.  Invite another participant to take your place.

**Commentary**   This is a popular game. So much so that participants do not like ending it. You may therefore wish to set a time limit before you start.

# Chains of Command

**Summary**   Participants examine their chain of command by constructing and labelling paper chains.

**Objectives**   Team-building (particularly through developing an understanding of organizational structure).

**Materials**   Strips of paper, coloured pens and glue.
Coloured wire (optional).

**Timing**   20 minutes.

**Procedure**
1. Invite participants to inscribe coloured strips with the names of people within their organization. Then invite them to glue the strips together in a paper chain to show their individual chain of command.
2. Take all the chains and invite participants to link them where there is an overlap (that is, through the same person featuring on several chains). They will in any event all link at the very top.
3. The completed chain (looking rather like a chandelier) can then be suspended from the ceiling. The coloured wire can be used to link people of the same level in the hierarchy and to hold the resulting mobile into shape.

**Commentary**   On a team-building course, the mobile can become a symbol of the group to be referred to at later points in the course. On an induction course it is a useful way of helping participants to picture themselves within the organization.

In organizations with a matrix structure (Handy 1985 p. 314, Kakabadse *et al.* 1987), this is a good way to explore the implications with a group.

**Variations**
1. The links can be in terms of seniority, experience, etc.
2. Mobiles based on different criteria can be constructed and compared.

# Chain Whispers

**Summary**  Passing a message via other people.

**Objectives**  Energizer.
Attention switching.
Introductions.

**Materials**  None.

**Timing**  Ten to 15 minutes.

**Procedure**
1. Ask participants to think of a message that they have for each of the other participants (it can be about their appearance, their clothes, their job, something they have said earlier in the course, and it can be a statement or a question). If they cannot think of something for each participant then they are not to worry; similarly, if they have more than one comment for one participant.
2. Ask them to ask another participant to pass the message to the target person along the lines of "could you please tell so-and-so that I like her dress?" If they have to find out the name of the intermediary on the way, then so much the better.
3. For the next round ask participants to use two intermediaries, then three. . . .

**Commentary**  This game can be processed if it is clear that messages have been distorted. It can also be used as a simple energizer or an introductions exercise (this latter is best just after an initial exchange of data).

**Variations**
1. Forbid participants to direct more than one question towards one other participant.
2. Ask that all the intermediaries should be different.
3. Give intermediaries the freedom to introduce other intermediaries.

# Chorus Line

**Summary**  Participants take turns in introducing themselves, and in seeing their introduction repeated in unison by the whole group.

**Objectives**  Introductions.
Self-disclosure.

**Materials**  None.

**Timing**  Five minutes (30 seconds per person).

**Procedure**
1. Form a circle. Explain that each person will introduce him or her self in a characteristic way (for example, hop, skip and jump, on one knee, singing in a funny accent). Give an example or two. On a count of three from yourself the others imitate it in unison.
2. Go round the circle.

**Commentary**  This should be done briskly and with enthusiasm. It is a useful way to help participants see their own actions reflected by others and gain a feel for the kind of impression they make on others, but in a non-threatening context.

# Class of their Own

**Summary**      Creativity exercise with a set of objects.

**Objectives**   Creativity.
Leadership.
Team-building.

**Materials**    Procedure sheets for group members.
Procedure sheets for leaders.
Procedure sheets for observers (optional).
Twenty small objects for each group, packaged in a parcel or put in a box. These should cover a wide variety of sources and material but be fairly common, and the same objects should be given to the two groups. A typical set of 20 would be:

> sachet of sugar substitute, clothes peg, ice cube tray, teabag, coin, button, compact disc, toothbrush, candle, fuse, bicycle pump nozzle, can opener, glass ashtray, paper clip, spark plug, thimble, mascara, empty match box, elastic band.

Pens and flipchart paper.
Separate rooms or working area for each group.

**Timing**       45 minutes.

**Procedure**    1.  Ask participants to form into groups of about five to eight people. The number of groups will vary with the number of participants.
2.  Ask the groups to choose a leader. Allocate the leaders to Type 1 (flexible) or type 2 (autocratic), but do not tell the group members at this point what the categories are. Give the leaders procedure sheets (on p. 29). Take questions from the leaders away from the other group members. Explain that, in addition to their own instruction sheet, the leaders have sheets for each of their team members.
3.  Allow the groups to complete their tasks in their separate rooms and put the resulting flipcharts up on the board. Show them

the different leaders' instructions on an overhead transparency. As a group, discuss if there is any significant difference between the types of group and the number of categories that they found. Consider the effects of competition on the working of the groups. Relate this to other situations where groups are asked to be flexible and creative.

**Commentary** This is a good exercise to run with two trainers, as it will be necessary to brief group leaders away from the main group. The observers (if there are any) are best briefed in the main group so that the other group members understand their role.

Issues that emerge are likely to include the relation between creativity and organization – too much of the latter inhibits the former. If the groups seem to function the same way then this can be used to explore group functioning. Why do we normally become so obsessed with structure when it does not seem to be necessary for this kind of work?

Emphasis on the learning points and on what group members felt from the exercise should prevent the members of the Group 2s from feeling that they have been "set up", which is a possible risk in this exercise.

**Variations** 1. Allow for the appointment of observers. This will require a further sheet for observers to use as a checklist (an example is given on p. 32). The observers will have to be given their own briefing.
2. If there is a large number of participants then groups of different sizes can be established to see what effect that has on creativity.

# Class of their Own –
# Instructions for Group 1 Leaders

**Group task** – to classify 20 objects in as many different ways as possible in ten minutes.

**Leader task** – to use as much as possible of the creative potential of all the group members.

**Method** –     put the objects on the table

pass out the instruction sheets

explain the group task

offer group members as much encouragement as possible

remind group members at intervals of what time they have left

# Class of their Own –
# Instructions for Group 2 Leaders

**Group task** – to classify 20 objects in as many different ways as possible in ten minutes.

**Leader task** – to channel the creative potential of the group so that it is focused on the task in hand and group members listen to each other properly. This role is crucial, as there is not enough time for you to take questions on your role and the way that the group is structured.

**Method** –    put the objects on the table

pass out the instruction sheets

explain the group task

check out that the group members have a clear and common understanding of the task and of what kinds of classification they could be thinking about.

chair the group efficiently so that people have a turn to be heard by all the other members of the group, and the resulting list of classifications is agreed by all the group members

ensure that group members are aware of how much time they have left at all times.

# Class of their Own –
# Instructions for Group Members

**Group task**

1. To think of as many different ways of classifying a group of objects as you can.

2. To put those classifications on newsprint with a total number at the end.

3. To complete the task in ten minutes.

# Class of their Own – Instructions for Observers

As observer your role is to not participate in the group but to observe what is happening. You will have an opportunity to report back at the end of the group session. Please do not intervene in the group except to call time after ten minutes have elapsed.

Pay particular attention to the following questions:

How did the leader act?

How did the group members respond to this?

What encouraged group members to be creative?

What discouraged group members from being creative?

How would you describe the atmosphere within the group?

How many people were active in the group discussion? How did this influence the effectiveness of the group?

Were there any times when the operation of the group really seemed to "change gear"? If so then describe them.

# Confessions of a Trombone Welder

**Summary**    Participants give themselves, and discuss, fantasy occupations.

**Objectives**    Introductions.

**Materials**    None.

**Timing**    15 minutes.

**Procedure**
1. Ask participants to invent a fantasy occupation for themselves (like trombone welding, for example).
2. Then ask each participant to introduce themselves to the group by name and occupation.
3. In a cocktail party atmosphere, spend five minutes milling around asking each other questions about their fantasy occupations, and taking great interest in the answers.

**Commentary**    You may wish to have a supply of occupations for your participants. They should be the sort of activities that *someone* must do, though nobody seems to know anyone who does them. Examples might be Ladder Lacquerer, Elephant Chiropodist, Mortuary Designer, Greetings Card Verse Writer, Knitting Needle Sharpener.

**Variation**    Participants can model fantasy garments (for example, stained glass socks).

# Continuum

**Summary**   Participants form each other and themselves into a line according to some quality or attribute.

**Objectives**   Energizer.
Self-perception.
Team-building.

**Materials**   None.

**Timing**   15 minutes minimum.

**Procedure**
1. Designate one end of the room *most* and one *least*.
2. Explain that you are going to rank the participants according to a category, with the most at one end and the least at the other. Then arrange them according to the category of your choice.
3. Then tell participants what the category is (for instance, how many staff you manage, how long you have had a driving licence, how much you've participated so far, how anxious you feel about this activity). The only limit is that *it should be a category on which each person can have their own unchallengeable view*.
4. Invite participants to change their position. Explain that nobody has the right to question anyone else's position. Eventually you should establish a continuum which all the participants are prepared to accept.
5. Invite participants to think of categories (like height, weight, hours of television watched in the past week, annual earnings, assertiveness, enthusiasm for the course, dominance within the group), and repeat Stages 2 to 4.

**Commentary**   Some people will use another person as a benchmark, some will have other ways of deciding where to put themselves, and these can be explored. Although the time taken to make the continuum is short, the consequent processing can take much longer and making (or appearing in) a continuum is a high risk activity. However, this way of confronting group members with the way that they perceive each other can be very powerful.

**Variations**
1. Start by having people place themselves in the continuum.
2. The game can be used to explore perceptions of more subjective qualities, as in **Domination** (p. 45).

# Creatriptych

**Summary**       A way of systematically solving problems by the geographical location and experiential anchoring of three aspects of problem solving activity.

**Objectives**    Problem solving (by separating creative, critical and pragmatic stages of developing a course of action).

**Materials**     Newsprint and pen.

**Timing**        20 minutes.

**Procedure**

*Preparation*   1.  Label a neutral position in the room where you feel secure and then three areas, Visionary, Pragmatist and Critic.
2.  Think of a time when you thought of some new ideas, or found a new way of doing something, or were creative. Step into the Visionary location and relive that experience using all your senses. Step out of Visionary and move back to Neutral.
3.  Think of a time when you were specific about how an idea was to be *practically* implemented, a time when you devised a specific plan. Step into the Pragmatist location and relive that experience using all your senses. Step out of Pragmatist and move back to Neutral.
4.  Think of a time when you criticised a plan or a proposal. Step into the Critic location and relive that experience using all your senses. Step out of Critic.

*Implementation*

5.  Pick an outcome you want to achieve.
6.  Step into Visionary, and in your mind and with your eyes closed run a movie of yourself accomplishing this goal. Just let the movie unfold as you watch. Step out and change state. Go back to Neutral if you wish.

7. Step into Pragmatist and check the plan you have dreamed up. Notice what you would need to change to make it more pragmatic. Step out and change state. Go back to Neutral if you wish.
8. Step into Critic and find out if anything is missing or needed. Step out and change state. Go back to Neutral if you wish.
9. Step back into Visionary and run a new movie which incorporates the new information from the pragmatist and the critic.
10. Cycle through Steps 7, 8 and 9 *until you are satisfied*.

**Commentary** This can be used for all participants at once or as a non-verbal exercise for those not taking an active part. Participants can do it individually and then discuss their feelings and result.

**Variation** This game can be effectively played in the open air.

# Creativity Quotient

**Summary**    Visual word identification game.

**Objectives**    Energizer.
Attention switching.

**Materials**    Prepared sheets (see below).
OHP (optional).
OHP slide of prepared sheet (optional).

**Timing**    15 minutes.

**Procedure**    1.    Hand out one of the prepared sheets (see pp. 39–40). Explain to the group that the figures represent ten words, phrases or expressions, and their task (as individuals) is to guess what they are.
2.    When they have worked them out, go round the group for the answers. Show a copy of the answer sheet on an overhead projector if desired.
3.    Ask the group to devise some examples of their own.

**Commentary**    Two question sheets have been included so that the game can be used on two different courses without the risk of participants remembering the answers that they had the previous time. This is a good energizer for a group in which some members have a mobility disability. It also fits well into any course where creativity or original thinking are being stimulated.

**Variation**    Collect the examples generated by the participants and use them to make further sets.

# Creativity Quotient – Test 1

|  |  |
|---|---|
| $\dfrac{\text{BUS}}{\text{BL}}$ | O<br>L I'M V<br>E |
| W<br>O<br>R<br>H<br>T | J<br>U<br>YOU S ME<br>T |
| $\underline{\text{HAND}}$ | R\|E\|A\|D\|I\|N\|G |
| L ᵥ ᴵ ᵢ ⱽ ₑ ᴱ ᵥᵥ | $\dfrac{\text{MAN}}{\text{BOARD}}$ |
| $\dfrac{\text{KNEE}}{\text{LIGHT}}$ | ART<br>HE |

# Creativity Quotient – Test 2

| | |
|---|---|
| HE'S HIMSELF | $\dfrac{\text{OATH}}{\text{UR}}$ |
| E<br>M<br>B | N<br>W<br>O<br>T |
| $\dfrac{\text{STAND}}{\text{I}}$ | L V E E L |
| ECNALG | $\dfrac{\text{O}}{\begin{array}{l}\text{Ph.D.}\\ \text{M.A.}\\ \text{B.Sc.}\end{array}}$ |
| POD<br>POD<br>POD | $\dfrac{\text{CRAZY}}{\text{V}}$ |

# Creativity Quotient – Answers

## Test 1

| | |
|---|---|
| BLUNDERBUS | I'M IN LOVE |
| THROW-UP | JUST BETWEEN YOU AND ME |
| HANDOVER PERIOD | READING BETWEEN THE LINES |
| LIVE INTERVIEW | MAN OVER BOARD |
| NEON LIGHT | BROKEN HEART |

## Test 2

| | |
|---|---|
| HE'S BESIDE HIMSELF | YOU ARE UNDER OATH |
| BEAM ME UP | UPTOWN |
| I UNDERSTAND | SPLIT LEVEL |
| BACKWARD GLANCE | THREE DEGREES BELOW ZERO |
| TRIPOD | CRAZY OVER YOU |

# Cutting Rose's Hair

**Summary**      Copying exercise.

**Objectives**   Non-verbal communication.

**Materials**    None.

**Timing**       Five minutes, and three minutes per person.

**Procedure**    
1. Explain that the next exercise is called "Cutting Rose's Hair", and then ask for a volunteer. All other group members should leave the room.
2. Explain to the person left that the objective of the game is to carry out a mime which will be copied by one other person in the group. This must be done without speaking. Explain that the mime you will do will be "Cutting a rose bush". Proceed to demonstrate this in detail, cutting off the dead heads collecting them, tying up loose branches, etc.
3. Invite another group member in and have the first do the mime for the second. Continue until all group members are back in the room.
4. Discuss how the mime has changed and why.

**Commentary** The mime should be done efficiently and in detail, but fairly briskly or the momentum of the game will be lost.

**Variation**    Allow the other people in to copy the mime individually and then send them out again without assembling the whole group until the very end of the game.

# Discriminet

**Summary**        Evaluation of similarities between different kinds of prejudice.

**Objectives**     Attributions.

**Materials**      Whiteboard.
Flipchart.
Pens.

**Timing**         30 minutes.

**Procedure**
1. Write up the grid on next page on a whiteboard. Introduce the seven categories of person (or the variations on them you have chosen) and the six qualities.
2. Ask the group to form syndicates to look at "commonly held beliefs" about one of the categories and write them up on the board.
3. When they have done this, ask the other groups to seek clarification or add to the comments where they can. You can probably draw connections between what has been put down for different categories. The attributions for "Irish" and "Black" may well be very similar, for example.
4. Reallocate the categories to different groups and ask them to demonstrate the fallacies in these generalizations and share them in the main group.

**Commentary**  This activity *must* be followed by one that fully undermines the stereotypes that may have been established.

**Variation**   The groups and the qualities can be varied as required.

| Discrimination Grid | | | | | | | |
| --- | --- | --- | --- | --- | --- | --- | --- |
| | Irish | Women | Blacks | Asians | Old People | Gays/Lesbians | Disabled |
| Intelligence | | | | | | | |
| Morals | | | | | | | |
| Beliefs | | | | | | | |
| Sex life | | | | | | | |
| Children | | | | | | | |
| What it's like having them visit | | | | | | | |

# Domination

**Summary**    Participants form each other and themselves into a line according to how dominant they feel they are.

**Objectives**    Assertiveness.
Self-perception.
Motivation.

**Materials**    None.

**Timing**    15 minutes.

**Procedure**
1. Designate one end of the room *most* and one *least*.
2. Ask for three volunteers, put one at each end of the room and one in the middle. Ask the others to line up in equal sized groups behind them.
3. Explain that they are categorized according to *dominance* and ask them to get themselves into the position they are happy with, by force if necessary.
4. Participants should then discuss their reactions. Bring out the fact that some people fought (that is, were dominant) to secure a *less* dominant position.

**Commentary**    Some people will use another as a benchmark, some will have other ways of deciding where to put themselves, and these can be explored. This is a variation of the game **Continuum** (p. 34).

**Variation**    A twist can be added with a decision making task for the group (for example, electing a group leader, choosing a name for the group, deciding on a start time for the next day) in which votes are distributed so that those who are least dominant are allocated the most votes (least dominant getting a number of votes equal to the number of group members, most dominant getting one vote, etc.). The group can then discuss the nature of leadership and what makes a good leader.

# Do You Come Here Often?

**Summary**    Simulation of party introductions.

**Objectives**    Listening skills.
Attributions.

**Materials**    Whiteboard and pens.
Co-trainer or accomplice.

**Timing**    20 minutes.

**Procedure**

1. Tell participants that they are to imagine that you are holding a cocktail party. You, the trainer, are the host, but you are so busy that all you have time to do is press a drink into the hand of the co-trainer/accomplice and introduce him/her to the participant saying "this is X——, I'm sure you two have a great deal in common. Excuse me . . ."
2. Ask participants to think about what questions they are going to ask to find out more about the person. Write them down on the whiteboard, separating out open and closed questions.
3. Explore the difference between the types of question. The handout on types of question (p. 48) may be helpful.

**Commentary**  Many of the questions that people suggest (including many of the classic "pick-up lines") are closed questions. I have found that in listening exercises course participants often fail to recognize this, giving one another incorrect feedback about the kind of questions they have actually asked.

The co-trainer/accomplice will have to decide in advance whether s/he is going to answer the questions that come out of this exercise. It can be useful if the accomplice has something to disclose which has not come out of the questioning.

**Variations**

1. Process what different questions might have been asked of a man or a woman.
2. Use yourself as the person to be talked to.

3. Role play the activity with half the group members (distinguished in some way, like by wearing a label) being observers, and writing down the questions asked by the person they are shadowing. (But see the risk noted above).

# Types of Question

**Open**        Where did you go for your holidays?

**Closed**      Did you go to Spain for your holidays?

**Multiple**    Did you go to Spain, Italy or France for your holidays, and when you went did you go as part of a package tour or not, and did you take your family?

**Reflecting**  So you were in France for your holiday. How did you like it? (reflecting and open)

**Directed**    Where did you go for your holiday, Moira?

**Rhetorical**  So, you're back from your holiday, then?

**Leading**     You *are* looking forward to your holiday, aren't you?

# Dracula has Risen from the Grave

**Summary**       Problem solving exercise in which no group has all the necessary information.

**Objectives**    Leadership.
                  Negotiation.
                  Problem solving.
                  Team-building.

**Materials**     Prepared cards for each group made according to the lists below.
                  Copies of the **Dracula has Risen from the Grave** scenario for each participant.
                  One copy of the **Dracula has Risen from the Grave Observer's Checklist** for each team.
                  Large copy of the **Dracula has Risen from the Grave Master Fact Sheet**.
                  Three working areas, with chairs and tables in them.

**Timing**        Two and a half hours.

**Procedure**     1.  Tell participants that they will be involved in solving a problem. Then ask them to form two teams of about equal size.
                  2.  Hand each person a copy of the scenario to read and ask them to elect a negotiator and an observer. Give the observers copies of their checklist.
                  3.  While the observers are reading their sheets hand out the cards to each group. The lists on pp. 51–56 show which cards go to which groups. Deal with any preliminary questions from the groups. At this stage make it clear that there is no penalty for submitting incorrect answers and rationales. Lead them to separate areas for the two groups, with neutral ground for the negotiators to meet which is large enough to also accommodate the observers.
                  4.  After an hour ask the participants to stop, even if no correct answers have been received. Allow 30 minutes for observers to

share with their groups what they saw, and invite team members to respond to this feedback.

5. In a plenary session ask the group to go through the rationale for the correct solution, drawing out the information that each group did not have. The **Dracula has Risen from the Grave Master Fact Sheet** shows which information each group had and the method for solving the problem.

6. Hold a discussion on:
   participants' reactions to sharing information in their team and needing information from the other team;
   how the exercise reflects what happens in other inter-group conflicts that participants have come across;
   what each team might have done differently to function better;
   how this can be applied to other groups.

**Variations**

1. Depending on numbers it might be necessary to have three groups, in which case the allocation of questions will have to be modified.

2. The nature of the problem is immaterial. Something more job-related could be used (such as the stages in the construction of a building, a chemical combination process, processing of documentation). The essential feature is that each group should have some of the elements necessary to make a series of logically connected statements in order to achieve a conclusion.

3. If some information is held back then this can also become an activity game with activities being allocated to groups as "payment" for further information. This will make for a much longer and more complicated game.

# Dracula has Risen from the Grave – Scenario

One of the lesser known effects of acid rain has been a change in the acidity of subsoils in Transylvania, which recently released poisonous gases into Castle Dracula. This has resurrected the Count, who is expected to take advantage of the improvement in East-West relations to resume his reign of terror in London. Your team's task is to kill him as soon as possible on his home ground. To do this your objective is *to establish the earliest day and time that you can kill the Count.*

You and your fellow team members will be given information that will help you to complete your task. However, other essential information will be held by the other team, with which your team is in competition (there being valuable film and publication rights to the ''I Killed Dracula'' story). The other team also need information which only you have. The only way that you can gain the other team's information is through your elected negotiator, who is to communicate directly and as often as necessary with the negotiator from the other team. Throughout this process the other team will be attempting to gain information from your team in the same way.

Your team must select *one* member to be your negotiator. Once that choice has been made, this role may not be assumed by any other person. Although observers are allowed to witness communications between the negotiators, other team members are not.

The winning team will be the one whose negotiator is the first to submit to the trainer *in writing* the correct name of the day and the time at which Count Dracula can be killed, *and* the correct rationale for the answer.

# Dracula has Risen from the Grave – Observer's Checklist

While the members of the group are working on their task your role is to observe them carefully. In addition, you are to observe the conversations between the negotiators. Throughout this observation period please provide answers to the following questions. Once the task has been completed you will then be asked to share your comments with the rest of the group, so please feel free to make notes in the space provided.

1.  How did the team approach the task?

2.  How did the members share information?

3.  What actions by group members hindered and helped the team in approaching its task?

4.  How did leadership emerge in the team?

5.  What signs were there of conflict in the group? How were they handled? Who by?

6.  How did team members react to their negotiator?

7.  How did the negotiator react to the rest of the group and to the other group's negotiator?

8.  How did the group members react to being in competition with another team?

9.  What was done to promote collaboration with the other team? Who by?

# Dracula has Risen from the Grave – Master Fact Sheet

COUNT DRACULA IS A VAMPIRE

COUNT DRACULA SLEEPS IN HIS TOMB

COUNT DRACULA'S TOMB IS IN THE CRYPT OF CASTLE DRACULA*

THERE IS NO DIRECT FLIGHT FROM ENGLAND TO TRANSYLVANIA

TODAY IS MONDAY

THE NEXT FLIGHT TO BUDAPEST IS AT 18.00 TONIGHT†

THE FLIGHT FROM LONDON TO BUDAPEST TAKES FIVE HOURS*

VAMPIRES CAN ONLY BE KILLED BY DRIVING AN OAK STAKE THROUGH THEIR HEART

OAK DOES NOT GROW IN TRANSYLVANIA*

OAK STAKES CAN ONLY BE BOUGHT AT THE BUDAPEST AIRPORT SHOP

THE BUDAPEST AIRPORT SHOP IS NOT OPEN THIS MONDAY OR TUESDAY DUE TO A LOCAL HOLIDAY†

THE PLANE FROM BUDAPEST TO TRANSYLVANIA LEAVES AT 14.00 ON TUESDAY AND THURSDAY AND TAKES ONE HOUR THE NEAREST RAILWAY STATION TO CASTLE DRACULA IS NOVAHUNY JUNCTION

THE TRAIN FROM TRANSYLVANIA AIRPORT TO NOVAHUNY JUNCTION TAKES SIX HOURS AND LEAVES THE AIRPORT AT 12.00 NOON ON FRIDAY, WEDNESDAY AND MONDAY

THE KEY TO THE CRYPT OF CASTLE DRACULA IS HANGING ON A NAIL IN THE VESTRY OF NOVAHUNY PARISH CHURCH WHICH IS BESIDE NOVAHUNY STATION

VAMPIRES CAN ONLY BE KILLED DURING DAYLIGHT†

NOVAHUNY PARISH CHURCH IS OPEN FROM SUNRISE TO SUNSET

THE SUN RISES IN TRANSYLVANIA AT 9.00 AND SETS AT 17.30

NOVAHUNY CHURCH IS 64 MILES FROM CASTLE DRACULA†

THE FASTEST YOU CAN TRAVEL TO THE CASTLE FROM THE CHURCH IS SEVEN MILES PER HOUR BECAUSE IT IS A ROCKY CROSS COUNTRY ROUTE AND YOU ARE CARRYING A LARGE OAK STAKE*

*not told to group 2
†not told to group 1

**Solution**     The earliest time you can kill Count Dracula is 9.00 on Sunday morning.

**Rationale for Solution**

1. Flying today (Monday) at 18.00, you will arrive at Budapest at 23.00 hours.
2. The oak stake you need to buy to the airport cannot be bought until Wednesday morning, which means the first flight you can get to Transylvania is the 14.00 Thursday.
3. You will arrive at Transylvania Airport at 15.00 Thursday. The next train is the Friday 12.00, arriving at Novahuny Junction at 18.00, half an hour too late to go to the church. The earliest you can get into the church is 9.00 Saturday.
4. It will take 9 hours to complete your walk to the castle, which means you will get there at 18.00 Saturday night, walking all day. This is too late to kill Dracula by daylight so you will have to wait until 9.00 Sunday morning.

# Dracula has Risen from the Grave – Fact Cards for Group 1

COUNT DRACULA IS A VAMPIRE

COUNT DRACULA SLEEPS IN HIS TOMB

COUNT DRACULA'S TOMB IS IN THE CRYPT OF CASTLE DRACULA

THERE IS NO DIRECT FLIGHT FROM ENGLAND TO TRANSYLVANIA

TODAY IS MONDAY

THE FLIGHT FROM LONDON TO BUDAPEST TAKES FIVE HOURS

VAMPIRES CAN ONLY BE KILLED BY DRIVING AN OAK STAKE THROUGH THEIR HEART

OAK DOES NOT GROW IN TRANSYLVANIA

OAK STAKES CAN ONLY BE BOUGHT AT THE BUDAPEST AIRPORT SHOP

THE PLANE FROM BUDAPEST TO TRANSYLVANIA LEAVES AT 14.00 ON TUESDAY AND THURSDAY AND TAKES ONE HOUR

THE NEAREST RAILWAY STATION TO CASTLE DRACULA IS NOVAHUNY JUNCTION

THE TRAIN FROM TRANSYLVANIA AIRPORT TO NOVAHUNY JUNCTION TAKES SIX HOURS AND LEAVES THE AIRPORT AT 12.00 NOON ON FRIDAY, WEDNESDAY AND MONDAY

THE KEY TO THE CRYPT OF CASTLE DRACULA IS HANGING ON A NAIL IN THE VESTRY OF NOVAHUNY PARISH CHURCH WHICH IS BESIDE NOVAHUNY STATION

NOVAHUNY PARISH CHURCH IS OPEN FROM SUNRISE TO SUNSET

THE SUN RISES IN TRANSYLVANIA AT 9.00 AND SETS AT 17.30

THE FASTEST YOU CAN TRAVEL TO THE CASTLE FROM THE CHURCH IS SEVEN MILES PER HOUR BECAUSE IT IS A ROCKY CROSS COUNTRY ROUTE AND YOU ARE CARRYING A LARGE OAK STAKE

# Dracula has Risen from the Grave – Fact Cards for Group 2

COUNT DRACULA IS A VAMPIRE

COUNT DRACULA SLEEPS IN HIS TOMB

THERE IS NO DIRECT FLIGHT FROM ENGLAND TO TRANSYLVANIA

TODAY IS MONDAY

THE NEXT FLIGHT TO BUDAPEST IS AT 18.00 TONIGHT

VAMPIRES CAN ONLY BE KILLED BY DRIVING AN OAK STAKE THROUGH THEIR HEART

OAK STAKES CAN ONLY BE BOUGHT AT THE BUDAPEST AIRPORT SHOP

THE BUDAPEST AIRPORT SHOP IS NOT OPEN THIS MONDAY OR TUESDAY DUE TO A LOCAL HOLIDAY

THE PLANE FROM BUDAPEST TO TRANSYLVANIA LEAVES AT 14.00 ON TUESDAY AND THURSDAY AND TAKES ONE HOUR

THE NEAREST RAILWAY STATION TO CASTLE DRACULA IS NOVAHUNY JUNCTION

THE TRAIN FROM TRANSYLVANIA AIRPORT TO NOVAHUNY JUNCTION TAKES SIX HOURS AND LEAVES THE AIRPORT AT 12.00 NOON ON FRIDAY, WEDNESDAY AND MONDAY

THE KEY TO THE CRYPT OF CASTLE DRACULA IS HANGING ON A NAIL IN THE VESTRY OF NOVAHUNY PARISH CHURCH WHICH IS BESIDE NOVAHUNY STATION

VAMPIRES CAN ONLY BE KILLED DURING DAYLIGHT

NOVAHUNY PARISH CHURCH IS OPEN FROM SUNRISE TO SUNSET

THE SUN RISES IN TRANSYLVANIA AT 9.00 AND SETS AT 17.30

NOVAHUNY CHURCH IS 64 MILES FROM CASTLE DRACULA

# Flattery

**Summary**    Negotiating the decoration and layout of a shared flat.

**Objectives**    Assertiveness.
Team-building.
Negotiation.
Attributions.

**Materials**    Prepared cards (optional).
Paper.
Pens.

**Timing**    30 minutes.

**Procedure**
1. Explain that participants have been given use of their employer's unfurnished flat for the indefinite future. They have £5000 with which to furnish and decorate it as they wish.
2. Ask them to write down a brief summary of what they will do, and a budget showing how they will spend the money.
3. Ask participants to add the four considerations which have been most important in coming to their decision (such as aesthetics, use of space, comfort, economy).
4. Explain that "owing to relocation within the company, the Managing Director has decided that you will have to share a flat with another person. That person is X—— (allocate a partner to each person). Now negotiate a plan for the flat which is acceptable to both of you."
5. Share the differences between people's initial and their final position, the process of negotiation that went on, and the extent to which the four considerations were met for each person.

**Variations**
1. If prejudice is being explored then participants can be given several prepared cards about the person they have to share with. They can be fairly full descriptions of people like and unlike group members in various respects, including such factors as being Chinese, deaf, blind, having a mobility disability,

gay, lesbian, of the same sex, of the opposite sex, 16 years old, 80 years old). They then have to negotiate that choice with another group member.

2. Vary the theme to include choosing a new team member, planning a holiday or buying a car.

# Fleet Street Fog

**Summary**        Game examining how understandable a passage of text is.

**Objectives**     Written communication.

**Materials**      A wide selection of newspapers (which do not have to be current). Prepared handouts (see below). Calculators. Whiteboard (optional). OHP (optional). Paper. Pens.

**Timing**         25 minutes.

**Procedure**
1. Explain that writing is often surrounded by a "fog" that makes the meaning hard to penetrate. Go through the Readability Index Sheet and explain how to carry out the calculation. Do so on a piece of text either written out on a whiteboard or put up on an overhead projector. It is useful to identify the punctuation and the three-plus syllable words by different colours.
2. Distribute newspapers and copies of the Readability Index Sheet and ask participants to work out some indexes for themselves. Ask them to try it several times on the same paper. Then invite them to try it on something they have written themselves.
3. Hold a discussion on the usefulness of the index and its reliability. Is a low score always appropriate? How can people use it to improve their own writing skills? Are there any kinds of writing where sentence length and word size are likely to be particularly difficult problems (such as report writing)?

**Commentary**  Other variations on the index exist (Noon 1985, pp. 97–8), but the one used here is well known. The calculation is a fairly easy one. It is useful to have previously calculated your own index and have it available.

**Variations**
1. Use recipes, advertisements, participants' own writing, instruc-

tion manuals, letters and other texts. The only kind of text you cannot properly use it for is something written in summary form without proper punctuation.

2. Vary the formula. You can include the number of meanings that a word has in the dictionary (ambiguity), number of non-English words, number of abbreviations, etc.

# The Readability Index

This index will give an idea of how many years of full time education in the English language a reader will need to understand a piece of writing.

1.  Take a section of text of exactly 100 words.
2.  Calculate the average sentence length, that is, 100 divided by the number of sentences.
3.  Calculate the number of words with three or more syllables. *Do not* count those beginning with a capital letter; those that are made from shorter words like "bookkeeper" or "housewife"; or those ending in "-es" or "-ed". Count all the others.
4.  Add the results of Stages 2 and 3 and multiply by 0.4. The result is the number of years of full time education in the English language a reader will need to understand a piece of writing.
5.  A rough guide to the kind of index which might be suitable for written work is as follows:

    | | |
    |---|---|
    | business memoranda | 8–10 |
    | business letters | 10–12 |
    | business reports | 12–14 |
    | business articles and books | 14–16 |

# Fruit Salad

**Summary**     A circle/centre game in which parts of the group are named after fruits.

**Objectives**     Energizer.
Attention switching.

**Materials**     A circle of chairs.

**Timing**     Five minutes.

**Procedure**
1.  Form the participants into a circle with yourself in the middle. Go round labelling all participants "apple" or "orange" (add more fruits for a large group, one fruit for each four people).
2.  Explain that you (whoever is in the middle) must ensure that a seat is vacated by another person. If you name a fruit then all those with that name must stand up and find a different seat. At "fruit salad" all must do this.
3.  Answer any questions, and carry out a trial run before running the game proper.

**Variations**
1.  Any other set of categories can be used.
2.  One variation known as "Stations" has each person named for a railway station. The person in the middle then says "I am going from X to Y" and can add intermediate stations. All those so named have to change places.

# The Game Game

**Summary**     Activity in which participants can choose to be competitive or co-operative.

**Objectives**  Team-building.
Decision making.
Assertiveness.
Negotiation.

**Materials**   Prepared sheets (see below).
Pens.
Counters, match-sticks, etc. (optional).

**Timing**      45 minutes.

**Procedure**   1.  Ask participants to form pairs and label themselves A and B. Tell them the following story:

> "I want you to imagine that each of you is one of a pair of male thieves. You have been arrested for burglary and put into separate cells. The police officer comes in to you and says "your friend has not yet confessed. But I am nevertheless prepared to make you an offer. If *you* confess and help me to convict him then I will ensure you get a light sentence. No more than seven days. I reckon he will get five years, though."
>
> You ask "what happens if both of us confess?"
>
> The police officer explains that you will both get a year in prison.
>
> You then ask "but what if neither of us confesses?"
>
> The police officer says, "well, to be frank with you, in that case I do not have enough evidence to convict either of you for burglary, and will have to charge you with breaking and entering – a month in prison each."

Ask if participants understand the story and clarify if necessary.

2. Hand out scoring sheets and counters to pairs, give them time to read and then take any questions. Do not guide them on the answers they should make, merely clarify the options, if necessary. Take them through the 20 games so that they are all making their moves at the same time so as to minimize conversation between partners.
3. When they have finished, discuss the strategies adopted. Display the payoff diagram. The discussion should consider

    (i)   What was most important, what you as an individual could gain (or avoid losing) and what pair of you could gain or avoid losing?

   (ii)   How did you feel about your partner and the effect of his or her actions on your losses?

  (iii)   How did you decide what your partner was going to do?

  (iv)   What real life situations raise these issues?

**Commentary** Counters make the game clearer for participants who are less experienced in dealing with numbers. The real life situations in which joint and individual payoffs are important include joint decision making (such as where to go on holiday), dis/rearmament, and when pedestrians cross the road into traffic. The discussion can serve as a starting point for an assertiveness session.

Sometimes there will be a demand for some input on the theory of games. You can refer to Meek (1972). Swenson (1973) and Buchler and Nutini (1969) offer more detailed background reading for yourself.

Given the element of conflict in this game, I would suggest that it be followed by an activity in which everyone co-operates.

The only reason that the thieves are male is because the story needs singular third person pronouns. For an all-female group this could be changed.

**Variations**
1. Use triads rather than pairs, with an observer keeping the score and contributing to the discussion.
2. Money or sweets can be used.
3. Teams rather than individuals can be used, and they can be asked to work in separate rooms.
4. The instructions can be written down.
5. Teams can be asked to predict each other's score at different points in the game.
6. Scores can be doubled, squared or otherwise modified at different points in the game to change the payoff.
7. Process observers can be appointed to teams.
8. Vary the payoffs for different pairs and discuss what effect this

has on competition and co-operation. It is possible to construct payoffs for a variety of situations, and the recommended reading will give some more examples. Matrices for three or more people can also be constructed, but they are harder to explain and represent. It would be possible to construct a whole course round the theory of games.

# Thief B

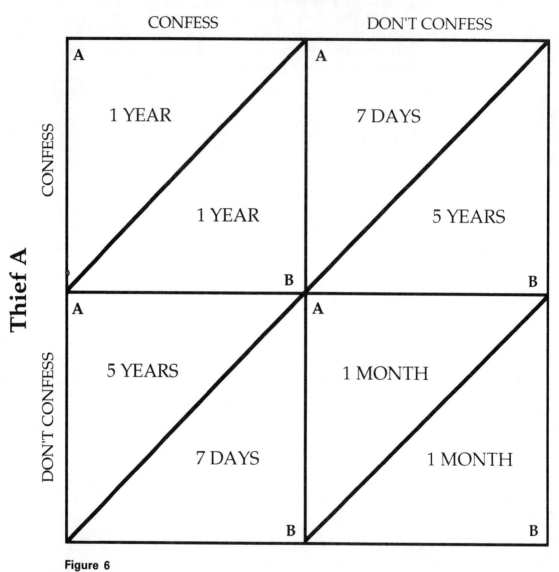

Figure 6

# Instruction Sheet for the Game Game

Your options are (i) to confess and (ii) not to confess. In these games please make a note of your move and then simultaneously disclose it to your partner. Score his or her action and the losses that the two of you have incurred.

*Do not talk to your partner except to exchange information on your moves.*

| | Games | Your action | Partner's action | Your loss | Partner's loss |
|---|---|---|---|---|---|
| 1. | | | | | |
| 2. | | | | | |
| 3. | | | | | |
| 4. | | | | | |
| 5. | | | | | |
| 6. | | | | | |
| 7. | | | | | |
| 8. | | | | | |
| 9. | | | | | |
| 10. | | | | | |
| 11. | | | | | |
| 12. | | | | | |
| 13. | | | | | |
| 14. | | | | | |
| 15. | | | | | |
| 16. | | | | | |
| 17. | | | | | |
| 18. | | | | | |
| 19. | | | | | |
| 20. | | | | | |

*Your total loss*

*Partner's total loss*

*Total joint loss*

# General Assembly

**Summary**     Assembly of shapes by a team.

**Objectives**  Team-building.
Non-verbal communication.
Negotiation.

**Materials**   Prepared card shapes in envelopes.
Instructions on flipchart.
Room with tables and chairs.

**Timing**      30 minutes.

**Procedure**
1. Form participants into groups of four or five around a table. Explain "your envelope contains parts of hexagons. In your group there are enough pieces to make up five hexagons of equal size. Your objective is to complete them. No person may have more than six pieces in front of them at one time. You can't talk or use sign language and you can't take other people's pieces or ask for a piece to be given to you."
Display a summary of these rules on the board.
2. Allow the game to proceed.
3. When the hexagons have been assembled hold a discussion. This can focus on:
   (i)   How do you communicate?
   (ii)  Did you try to work as a team? How?
   (iii) How did people help or obstruct each other?
   (iv)  Did you have leaders? How did they operate?

**Commentary** This is a simple exercise which requires co-operation within a group, and it is particularly suitable for team-building courses.

**Variations**
1. If the numbers leave you with a few left then hold the game in "fishbowl" form with a group of observers round the outside.
2. Use other shapes and patterns.
3. Remove the restriction on non-verbal communication.

# General Assembly

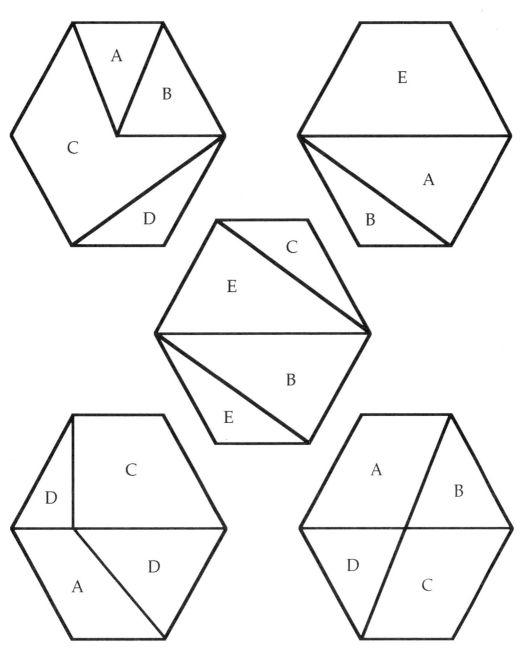

**Figure 7**

# Go-Go

**Summary**     Competition energizer based on the Japanese board game of Go.

**Objectives**  Energizer.
Attention switcher.

**Materials**   Metronome.
Something to identify a team (like an armband).

**Timing**      Ten minutes.

**Procedure**   1.  Ask the group to form into two teams. Place them equally spaced at opposite ends of the room.
2.  Explain that they may only move in time with the metronome. Their objective is to remove rival players from the floor by three of them touching him/her at the same time. A player may only be touched by an enemy if s/he is being touched by fewer than four friends (total touching are four).

**Commentary** The metronome speed can be varied as required.

# Goodies

**Summary**    Exploring positive qualities of group members.

**Objectives**    Assertiveness.
Self-disclosure.
Team-building.

**Materials**    Pens and paper.

**Timing**    20 minutes.

**Procedure**

1. Ask participants to think of four "goodies" about themselves. These can be abilities, feelings or attitudes, but they should not relate directly to possessions. Ask them to consider

   (i) What is the goodie?
   (ii) How and where was it demonstrated?
   (iii) What were the consequences)

   Signal that you will be asking them to talk briefly about their findings.
2. Run the discussion on the basis of free disclosure (people can say what they wish about themselves but there should be no questioning or challenging).
3. Lead this into a free discussion covering
   (i) How people feel about saying good things about themselves.
   (ii) How the exercise makes them feel about themselves.
   (iii) For team-building, what implications this has for our working as a team

**Commentary**  In courses other than team-building it is best if the trainer participates. You may wish to comment on the way we regard compliments as if they have to be swapped. There is no reason why they cannot be just given. This game can be linked to **Resents and Appreciates** (p. 117) if it is used in the course. If it is then it is best to play Goodies on the first day.

**Variation**     On team-building courses the goodies should be related to the working environment.

# Gripes Auction

**Summary**     A simulated auction of gripes.

**Objectives**  Team-building.
Self-disclosure.

**Materials**   Flipchart and pens.

**Timing**      20 minutes.

**Procedure**   1.  Ask the group to consider and then shout out their "gripes". These can relate to work (best for a workplace team-building exercise), or to any aspect of life: put them up on the board. Participants can make more than one suggestion. Give the group members an amount of money (like £100), and proceed to auction off the gripes. They are to buy in as many of their hates as possible, or to concentrate on securing the one(s) that matter most to them. Only one of each item will be sold, and this will go the highest bidder.
2.  Proceed to auction. If nobody bids for an item then pass on to the next one. Then discuss why people bought what they did, and encourage others to put their point of view.

**Variations**  Make it a "Loves Auction". Restrict the gripes/loves to Attitudes, Things People Say, People I Know, or other categories. For groups of younger people you can use play money.

**Commentary**  A version of this game is the first stage of **Sixty-Second Solos** (p. 123).

# Grouptalk

**Summary**    Validation committee of group members.

**Objectives**   Assertiveness.
Leadership.
Team-building.
Written communication.
Validation.
Expectations.
Action planning.

**Materials**    Chairs set round table for groups of 5–8 in separate rooms.
Chairs for observer (optional).
Paper and pens.
Prepared agenda (example below).

**Timing**    20 minutes or longer.

**Procedure**

1. Ask participants to form a full committee (or committees of 6–8 if it is a large group) to discuss how the course is proceeding. The meeting should be conducted with *some* formality to the extent of having a written agenda, a Chair and a Secretary. You may wish to offer brief input at this point on the role of the Chair, the Secretary, agenda and minutes. Ask that the meeting be conducted at such a pace that the Secretary will be able to provide a readable set of minutes to the trainer at the end of the meeting. Answer any questions that participants have. Mention that trainers will be observing if this is the case.

2. Have rooms set out in committee format with agendas at each place. If desired, have chairs set out at the side for the trainer(s) to observe. The content of the agenda will be determined by the nature of the course, but an illustrative agenda from a development course for clerical staff is given below.

3. Allow the committee to work through the agenda. Do not interfere with the progress of the meeting or participate unless asked. A stopwatch can be used to time the meeting, and the

trainer might focus on the skills being used by participants (listening skills, assertiveness) as appropriate to the course.

4. Either at the end of the meeting or on the following day, offer feedback to the Chairs and the Secretaries. Self-criticism and feedback from the groups will often be enough, but another way of making this positive is to ask the Chair and Secretary what advice they have for their successor. You may wish to process other matters then, such as whether the Chairs are always chosen from the men in the group and the Secretaries from the women. If there are more than one group then this processing can take place either in the main groups or before the meetings of the separate committees.

**Commentary** This is a good end-of-day exercise. In practice the participants forget the presence of the trainer very soon and think about the task in hand. Carried out at the end of the day it provides useful validation of course content and participant attitudes to it, as well as information on expectations for the following day's activities. Often, feelings about the course are vocalized which never find their way into the minutes, but which an alert trainer can pick up. If two groups are used then it is important to prevent feelings of competition or inferiority to arise, and one way of doing this is by carrying out feedback in the separate groups.

If two groups are used then members can be exchanged through the duration of the course.

I have found this activity particularly successful with groups of participants who do not usually have the opportunity to practise meeting skills at work.

For some reason, participants tend to take the game more seriously if they are seated round a high table in proper "committee" style than if they are seated in their normal horse-shoe or round a low table.

**Variations** The agenda can be provided only to the Chair and Secretary.

A time constraint can be set to either the whole agenda or to parts of it (see example below).

Other topics for Item 7 of the agenda might be dog licensing, tobacco advertisements, car and lorry bans in inner cities and disabled access to public buildings. They should be topics on which everyone is likely to have a view, and which will not be restrained by lack of information. Avoid topics like religion and the death penalty.

# Sample Agenda

1.  Select a Chair and Secretary for the meeting.*
2.  Agree the minutes of the last meeting.
3.  Choose a name for your group.*
4.  Today in this course you discussed   Assertiveness
                                          Working in Groups

    What did you learn?
    How can you apply it back at work?
5.  Tomorrow we shall be discussing   Interviewing Skills
                                      Presentational Skills

    What *specific* questions would you like answered on these topics.†
6.  Next Monday you will be confronted by your usual in tray. In coping with your work what will you do differently as a result of this course?
7.  Your Managing Director has asked your Committee for recommendations on the introduction of a smoking policy for open planned offices, traditional offices, canteens, rest rooms, waiting rooms and interview rooms in your company. Agree a series of recommended policies, taking no longer than 15 minutes.
8.  Elect a different Chair and Secretary for the next day.
9.  Any other business.

*these items are only needed on the first day.
†this item is only needed on the last day.

# Helping Hands

**Summary**        An activity in which participants learn to massage each other's hands.

**Objectives**     Trust.
                   Non-verbal communication.
                   Stress management.

**Materials**      None.

**Timing**         25 minutes.

**Procedure**      1.  Ask what connotations massage has for group members, and explore the negative ones. Explain the benefits that massage can offer. It can improve circulation, relax muscles, aid digestion, stimulate lymph and thereby help remove toxins from the body. There are psychological benefits and evidence that massage reduces the blood pressure of the person giving it. Offer hand massage as a simple way of feeling the benefits of massage without evoking any of the seedy connotations that massage has.
                   2.  Invite participants to choose a partner and label themselves A and B. Then tell them which will be the masseur and which the subject.
                   3.  Ask the pair to sit comfortably facing each other. The masseur should sit relatively upright and the subject can close her or his eyes. Model this with a member of the group.
                   4.  Go through the stages of massage:

                       Hold the hand palm down in one of your hands, stroke firmly down the fingers one by one.

                       Squeeze the fingers all down their length.

                       Press gently with the thumb on each of the finger joints, being careful to support it with the other hand at all times.

Grip the fingers one by one between two of your clenched fingers and gently shake the finger like a dog worrying a bone.

Massage the palm from the inside with your knuckles.

Returning to your first position, stroke with your thumbs from the knuckles to the wrist up the web between the fingers.

Hold the hand in your hand and move it about, while the other person allows the fingers to go limp. Get as much a feel for the different muscles and the way that they move over one another as you can.

Gently unfolding the hand with both of yours, stroke with your thumbs out from the centre of the palm.

Supporting the hand with your fingers stroke the wrist all over with your thumbs, moving them away from each other as they work down away from the hands.

Finally, stroke the whole hand all over, ending by sandwiching it between your fingers for a couple of seconds and then letting it go and resting it on the leg or body of the subject.

5. Ask participants how they felt about the exercise. Masseurs first and then subjects. If there is time then invite them to change roles.

**Commentary** Ensure that you are quite familiar with the movements involved before you go through them with a course. Remember that this game requires enough trust for physical contact to be possible between course members. In practice this is not usually a problem (the hand being one of the least threatening parts of the body to be touched), but participants should be able to opt out if they so wish. You will usually find that subjects want the other hand to be massaged too. There are many books on massage to which you can refer participants for more information but I would particularly recommend Maxwell-Hudson (1988). You may also wish to refer them to local classes on the subject.

**Variation** If your group wants a follow-up exercise to this it would be possible to devise a similarly effective foot or face massage from the source indicated.

# If Eggs could Fly

**Summary**    Teams compete to drop an egg a stated distance.

**Objectives**    Teamwork.
Leadership.
Creativity.
Problem solving.

**Materials**    Tape measure.
Two sheets of A4 paper for each team.
Two hen's eggs for each team.
Two round balloons for each team.
Twelve inches of sellotape for each team.
Three feet of string for each team.
Instruction sheets.
Video equipment (optional).
Chairs for each team.
Tables for each team with the materials on them (but only one egg).

**Timing**    70 minutes (100 if video used).

**Procedure**    1.    Ask participants to arrange themselves into teams of 5–6 people. Explain that they will be given a task to complete in their groups, and that they will have 30 minutes in which to complete it. Separate the teams out round their prepared tables and give them their task sheets. Ask the groups to return to the tables when holding discussions of their solutions. If there are any questions then refer the questioners to the instruction sheet. Begin to time them. Run a video of each group and note the time of significant events.
2.    At the end of the half hour period (after a break if preferred) ask the groups to demonstrate their solutions to the problem.
3.    Ask the groups what they learned about themselves while carrying out the exercise. Focus first on how a solution was reached and use video (if made) to demonstrate roles takes by group members (for example, Leader, Critic, Developer, Pragmatist,

Inventor, or by reference to a team roles inventory such as Benne and Sheats (in Adair 1983), Belbin (1981) or Margerison and McCann (1990)). Then focus on the feelings that the exercise evoked, and how much of themselves group members invested in the task. Then discuss how what was learned can be applied back at work.

**Commentary** It should go without saying that the solution itself is immaterial to the success of the training exercise. However, I have had colleagues ring me long distance in the middle of a course for the 'right answer'! I have seen the same solution succeed and fail, depending on the pile of the carpet, the thickness of the eggshell or just luck.

It is a good idea to keep your own comments to a minimum before the exercise starts. The break will be necessary if video is used to allow the trainer time to decide which parts of the video to show. A video with a counter will be useful. If video is not used then a minute by minute assessment of what is happening in the group is useful, possibly with a digital stopwatch counting them down. Ideally one trainer is needed for each group. Reminders can be given to the group if necessary.

**Variations**
1. Time penalties can be imposed for questions asked of the trainer.
2. The element of competition can be made more or less important by the way that the groups are treated. It is even possible to draft the instruction sheet to state that the team that finishes first will be the winner. Alternatively, groups can be encouraged to share resources.
3. The whole exercise can be costed in terms of time, resources, advice from trainer, etc., as suggested for **Babel** (p. 15).
4. The resources can be changed (100 paper straws and a gallon can of water perhaps), or the task modified, perhaps to suspending *two* eggs.
5. Other tasks which can form the basis for a similar exercise are:

   – placing a bomb (represented by a tennis ball) inside a drum of water in a specified time without going closer than four feet to the ball (or it will explode);
   – the heaviest member of the group has to touch the ceiling with nose and toes at the same time for a continuous period of two minutes;
   – moving the contents of a bucket of water to another bucket without moving either, using only material in the room in a set time.

# If Eggs could Fly Task

Your team's task is to drop a raw hen's egg from a height of at least ten feet directly to the floor without breaking or damaging the egg in any way on impact.

Your resources are as follows:

2 sheets A4 paper
1 hen's egg
12″ of sellotape
2 balloons
3′ of string.

Your time limit is 30 minutes, after which time the task should be demonstrated in front of the trainer.

A further egg will be available for demonstration purposes only at the end of the exercise.

# If I Were You

---

**Summary**    Individuals act out how they think their partner would behave in a certain situation.

**Objectives**    Self-perception.
Feedback.
Non-verbal communication.
Team-building.
Assertiveness.

**Materials**    None.

**Timing**    25 minutes.

**Procedure**
1. Divide the group into pairs and ask them to label themselves A and B.
2. B is to act out how A would act in a certain situation (examples below). They have ten minutes in which to discuss it.
3. B receives guidance from A on how A would really act, and modifies his or her actions accordingly.
4. Participants reverse roles.
5. Discuss the experience in pairs and then in the main group. Focus on the appropriate learning points.

**Variations**    The situations can be elicited from the group in a brainstorming session.

**Situations**    How someone acts on the phone when they get an abusive wrong number.
How someone enters a meeting or social situation late.
How someone reacts to the possibility of unwanted in-laws visiting for a public holiday.
How someone returns goods to a shop and demands a refund.
How someone replies to a friend who has brought some awful clothes about whether you really like them.
How someone breaks bad news to a friend.

How someone behaves during an argument with someone they are fond of.

How someone complains about an over-cooked steak in a restaurant.

How someone admits that they were wrong.

How someone behaves making a difficult decision about where to go on holiday.

How someone reacts when asked by a friend to lend a large sum of money.

How someone reacts to being given a good/bad staff report.

How someone returns stale beer in a pub.

# In the Neck

**Summary**    Participants massage each other's necks.

**Objectives**    Stress management.
Trust.
Non-verbal communication.

**Materials**    None.

**Timing**    15 minutes.

**Procedure**
1. Form participants in a circle and ask them all to face the same way so that they are facing each other's backs.
2. Ask them to put their hand loosely on the shoulders of the person in front of them. Then proceed to gently massage their shoulders and neck. Encourage those massaged to show by noises and gestures what they do and do not enjoy.
3. Suggest that they all turn round and massage the other way.

**Commentary**  This game requires enough trust for physical contact to be possible between course members. In practice this is not usually a problem. Members should be able to opt out if they so wish, though.

# It's Not Fair!

**Summary**      A competitive game in which resources are allocated unequally to groups.

**Objectives**   Team-building.
Negotiation.

**Materials\***  Prepared task sheets.
Two reels sellotape.
Three sheets 10″×10″ blue paper.
Three sheets 10″×10″ yellow paper.
Compass and ruler.
Tables and chairs arranged so that the groups can be seated
separately.
10″×10″ sheet of silver foil.
Three sheets 10″×10″ white paper.
Three sheets 10″×10″ red paper.
Glue and scissors.
(\*many of these items will have to be packaged before the game
commences – see below)

**Timing**       About one hour.

**Procedure**   1.   Allocate participants to groups, sit them round their tables and
distribute packaged resources and task sheets. With four groups
the allocation for the task sheet reproduced here might be:

| *Group 1* | *Group 2* |
|-----------|-----------|
| sellotape | sellotape |
| silver foil | compass |
| 1 yellow sheet | 2 red sheets |
| 1 white sheet | 1 yellow sheet |
| | 1 white sheet |

*Group 3*
scissors
1 white sheet
2 blue sheets
1 yellow sheet

*Group 4*
glue
1 blue sheet
2 red sheets
ruler

2. Explain that each group has different materials, but that each group will be asked to complete the same tasks. There is enough material in total to achieve all of the tasks if it is used in a certain way. The groups may bargain for the use of materials in any way they wish. The first group to complete all the task will be declared the winner. There is no time constraint.
3. While the tasks are being completed observe as much of the proceedings as possible, but try not to be drawn into interpreting the instructions or suggesting solutions. Try to take an active part if assigned a specific task.
4. When the task has been completed by one group, initiate a discussion on the extent of co-operation and competition that existed, the bargaining that went on and sharing feelings.

**Commentary** You will have to decide on a task, a number of groups and the allocation of resources within those groups before introducing the task. The allocation should be unequal, but not so unequal that one group feels too demoralized to attempt the tasks. You may need to strip the rooms used of other materials that might be used to complete the tasks.

**Variations**

1. Have some of the participants serve as observers, and give structured feedback.
2. Leave objects around that could be used but that are not part of the "official" material.
3. Vary the resources and the tasks.

# Task Sheet

Your group is to complete all of the following tasks:

1. Make a cube of silver foil with sides 2″×2″×2″.
2. Make a paper aeroplane at least 20″ long which flies.
3. Make a flag of 3″×5″ in at least three colours.
4. Make a red hexagon with sides 2″ long.
5. Make a paper chain of at least three colours.

# Knots

**Summary**      Exercise in relaxation through untying each other.

**Objectives**   Stress management.
Trust.

**Materials**    None.

**Timing**       15 minutes.

**Procedure**    1.   Ask participants to form two groups. One group is to lie on the floor with some space around them. Ask them to form themselves into a knot and then to close their eyes until told to open them.
2.   Ask the members of the second group to select a person and to gently unravel them and put them into as comfortable a position as they can. The aim is to make it as easy as possible to relax.
3.   Ask the "sleepers" to open their eyes, and then to discuss how they found the experience and how their partners might have made it better for them.

**Commentary**   This game requires enough trust for physical contact to be possible between course members. In practice this is not usually a problem. Members should be able to opt out if they so wish, though.

# Learnabout

**Summary**    Introductions through self-disclosure and repetition.

**Objectives**    Introductions.
Self-disclosure.
Energizer.

**Materials**    Small object (for instance, a tennis ball).

**Timing**    One minute per person.

**Procedure**    1. Form participants into a circle and explain that you will be giving them the opportunity to learn a few things about each other. Explain that whoever has the ball should throw it to someone else, who should say their name and then disclose anything about themselves which has not been revealed yet. Keep the examples unthreatening (such as "I am wearing contact lenses", "I have a dog").
    2. When everyone has had a turn explain that in the second round people will have to throw the ball at someone, say *that person's* name and what they have said about themselves. The person spoken about can prompt if necessary.

**Commentary**    This is a useful first afternoon energizer when participants know a little about one another and are probably ready to share more.

**Variation**    In the second round participants can be asked to repeat everything that has been said up to that point.

# Legover

**Summary**     A communication exercise in describing how to make an object.

**Objectives**   Feedback.
Non-verbal communication.

**Materials**    Lego bricks.
Wrapping paper.

**Timing**       20 minutes.

**Procedure**
1. Ask for a volunteer from the group. Give a wrapped and completed lego figure to that person and designate them the speaker.
2. Give the lego bricks to the other participants.
3. Explain that the speaker must manage the construction of a duplicate figure by the rest of the group. The speaker has to face away from the group as if communicating instructions by telephone.
4. In a second round (with a different speaker and set of bricks) the speaker *is* allowed to see the results of his or her instructions.
5. Discuss the difference between the two situations. Bring out the role of non-verbal communication and feedback in ensuring that a message is properly received.

**Variations**
1. If the task is being used to explore closed questions then the speaker remains out of sight, can be asked questions but can only give one word answers.
2. A similar exercise can be carried out in pairs, one partner drawing a pattern described by the other as they sit back to back.

# Lemon and Lime

**Summary**    Introductions exercise using fruit leading into examination of prejudice.

**Objectives**    Team-building.
Introductions.
Attributions.

**Materials**    Fresh fruit (lemon or lime) for each group member.

**Timing**    20 minutes.

**Procedure**
1. Hand out a fruit to each person and ask them to "get to know your fruit".
2. Ask participants to choose a partner and introduce their fruit to that person, sharing what they have discovered about it.
3. Divide the group into Lemons and Limes on the basis of their fruit. Put them into separate rooms, and invite them to think of as many ways in which their fruit is "better" than the other group's.
4. Bring the two groups together, and ask them in turn to say why they thought they were better.
5. If relevant, speak briefly about the nature of prejudice and labelling theory. Make the point that compared to other fruits lemons and limes are far more similar than different. Reconcile the groups by asking members to squeeze their fruit out and by using the juice to make a drink for later in the course.

**Commentary**  A good introduction to the psychology of person-perception is to be found in Lloyd and Mayes, 1984, pp. 629–39.

    Lemons and limes were chosen because they are two fruits which seem rather similar on the surface. They also can't be eaten during the first stage of the exercise!

**Variations**    The two stages of the exercise can be separated, or only one used if this better meets the learning objectives.

# Little Attentions

**Summary**    Exercise in listening and not listening.

**Objectives**    Non-verbal communication.
Listening skills.

**Materials**    Chair.

**Timing**    15 minutes.

**Procedure**
1. Form participants into pairs (A and B) and ask them to get their chairs more or less facing each other. Explain that the As are going to be speakers and the Bs listeners.
2. Explain that the As are to speak about "What I did last night" (enlivened or expurgated if necessary) for two minutes, and that the Bs are to do anything but listen. The only bar on them is that they cannot leave the room.
3. As they do so encourage the listeners to not listen. Then hold a discussion on

   (i) What the listeners were doing to show that they were not listening.
   (ii) How the speakers knew that they were not being listened to.
   (iii) How they felt about the exercise.

   Lead into the subject of listening skills if required.

**Commentary** This exercise can lead into general considerations of listening skills. It is a brief and usually very successful exercise, although you should take care that it is not used on too many different courses in which the same people might take part.

**Variation**    The pairs can be seated or standing back-to-back or side-to-side, or lying next to each other. The differences these positions make can then be explored.

# Lost for Words

**Summary**    Communication exercise using minimal vocabulary.

**Objectives**    Non-verbal communication.
Listening skills.
Energizer.

**Materials**    Pens.

**Timing**    30 minutes.

**Procedure**
1. Ask participants to choose the ten words which they would keep if they had to lose all the others in their language.
2. Then ask them to choose three out of those ten which they will keep.
3. Ask them to mill around and hold conversations with a partner using only their three words, but to convey as much as they can.
4. Ask them to change partners a couple of times.
5. Discuss as a group what they were able to communicate and how they managed it.

**Commentary**    Going from ten to three (Stage 2) is a good way to ensure participants focus on the things that are most important to them. It can be applied to other training games. If it is acceptable to the group, video-recording this exercise can be very useful if group members are allowed to discover facts about their non-verbal repertoire from studying the tape. This can be done by following the group round with a shoulder mounted camera.

**Variation**    Use gestures rather than words, or place constraints on both.

# The Missing Link

**Summary**      Communication exercise for a whole group.

**Objectives**   Team-building.
Non-verbal communication.
Decision making.

**Materials**    Pens and paper.
Prepared cards for each person.
Movable chairs for each person.

**Timing**       20 minutes.

**Procedure**    1.  Form the group into circles of about six people and arrange them in a circle facing outwards so that they are not able to see each other. Hand out prepared cards (see p. 96).
2.  Explain that the card has six words on it. All the cards have one feature in common. Their task is to discover what that is. The rules are that

    (i)   They are not to speak to each other.
    (ii)  They are not to show their card to another group member.
    (iii) They may communicate only by writing notes to each other.
    (iv)  The notes are to have no more than four of the words on them.

3.  When the task has been completed, hold a discussion on how people felt and how they acted as a group. Ask what they might do differently if they were confronted with the situation again.

**Commentary**   Be sure to include some false clues (that is, rules followed by all but one of the cards). In this instance the rule is that each word on each card rhymes with one word on each of the other cards.

94

**Variations**
1. The task can be based on numbers, random sets of letters or abstract patterns rather than words.
2. Base the task on playing cards or on dominoes – either real or on cards.
3. Vary the level of difficulty of the question (from the number of vowels on the cards always being a prime number (difficult) to the selections all being anagrams (easy)).

# The Missing Link

| | | |
|---|---|---|
| SMOKE | DATE | PIE |
| RELY | DISPERSE | FOLK |
| MOON | SILT | TUNE |
| PURSE | SPOON | CURSE |
| RELATE | BLOKE | SPILT |
| GUILT | DENY | ABATE |

| | | |
|---|---|---|
| SOAK | INVOKE | CRY |
| MY | PLATE | TILT |
| MATE | WILT | CLOAK |
| IMMUNE | SKY | NURSE |
| IMMERSE | WORSE | GOON |
| GUILT | BOON | ESTATE |

**Figure 8**

96

# Mommie Said . . .

**Summary**      Cocktail party simulation exploring parental messages.

**Objectives**   Team-building.

**Materials**    None.

**Timing**       20 minutes.

**Procedure**
1. Invite participants to think about one of their parents (it does not matter if they are still alive or not). Encourage them to think about the voice, manner, and so forth, of that person, and then to imagine that parent thinking about them, in the present if that is possible, and to imagine what those thoughts are.
2. Invite them to mingle and talk to each other about themselves as if they were that parent talking about them.
3. In a general discussion, ask participants to consider the extent to which they ever felt an internal message saying what they have said about themselves and acted upon it. Make reference to defence mechanisms (Freud 1936) or transactional analysis (Stewart and Joines 1987), as appropriate.

**Variations**
1. Other authority figures or people in the group can be used.
2. The subject's child, lover, worst enemy, etc., can be used.
3. Participants can be given a free choice and others asked to guess whose view of the person is being represented.

# Naked City

**Summary**      Group members act as a team to complete a series of tasks based on places in their city.

**Objectives**   Team-building.
Leadership.
Presentational skills.
Problem solving.

**Materials**    Access to a public service telephone.
Prepared Ordnance Survey maps showing the locations given in the task sheet for each group (this makes the task harder than using street maps).
Prepared task sheets for each group.
Compass for each group.
Three one-day public transport travel cards (or local equivalent) for each group.

**Timing**       Variable, depending on tasks used (for the sheet on p. 100, 3 hours for an eight person team with a further two hours for processing).

**Procedure**    1. Ask participants to arrange themselves into teams of no more than eight people. It is preferable to have one group only, and this will be possible if the number of tasks is varied. If there are one or two over the eight then some group members can be asked to serve as observers on the others. They can then be swapped over during the exercise.
2. Explain that each group will be asked to carry out a number of tasks. They will be given no further guidance on how to carry out these tasks. Explain that there is a non-negotiable time limit of three hours on the completion of the tasks. Hand out the task sheets.
3. Monitor the groups (one trainer to each group) as they go about their tasks.
4. Ask the groups to present their findings. Then ask them what they learned about themselves while carrying out the exercise.

Focus first on how the tasks were allocated, which (if any) tasks were not attempted, and how tasks were prioritized and allocated to group members. Demonstrate roles taken by group members (for example, Leader, Critic, Developer, Pragmatist, Inventor). Then focus on the feelings that the exercise evoked, and how much of themselves group members invested in the task. Then discuss how what was learned can be applied back at work.

**Commentary** It is a good idea to keep your own comments before the exercise starts to a minimum. The content of the activity should be processed before examining the dynamics of the group. In that way, the work done is fully acknowledged. Stage 4 also allows for the exercise of presentational skills. The emphasis on this will depend on the objectives of the training event. This game is based on the same principles as **Picture Hunt** (p. 109).

**Variations**
1. Time penalties can be imposed for questions asked of the trainer.
2. The element of competition can be made more or less important by the way that the groups are treated. It is even possible to draft the instruction sheet to state that the team that finishes first will be the winner.

# Sample Task Sheet

The tasks below should be completed by your group in the time allowed. Please advise the trainer in writing if any member of the team leaves the building, explaining where they are going.

## Tasks

1.  RUSSELL SQUARE – how many hotels front onto the square? What are their names?
2.  BROADCASTING HOUSE – who made the statue over the entrance. What is it called?
3.  HYDE PARK – produce a postcard of the Peter Pan statue in Hyde Park.
4.  SCIENCE MUSEUM – what are the opening times?
5.  510 BUS ROUTE – what is the make and model of bus used on this route?
6.  HARRODS – produce a plastic carrier bag.
7.  SERPENTINE BOAT HOUSE – what is for hire? What are the opening times?
8.  SELFRIDGES – receipt with today's date on it and a plastic carrier bag.
9.  DORCHESTER HOTEL – how many single rooms? How much is a double room with and without *en suite* facilities?
10. VICTORIA COACH CENTRE – how many bus bays are there? If you were travelling to Bristol, which bay would you go to?
11. QUEEN MOTHER SPORTS CENTRE – how much is the annual membership fee? What facilities are on offer?
12. WESTMINSTER ABBEY – what are the opening times? What time is there free access? Produce a postcard of the Abbey.
13. GREEK STREET – how much does a rum and coke cost at the Gay Hussar?
14. NEW ZEALAND HOUSE – what immigration restrictions are there on UK nationals?
15. AUSTRALIA HOUSE – what immigration restrictions are there on UK nationals?
16. CANADA HOUSE – what immigration restrictions are there on UK nationals?
17. BUSES – how many seats are there on the upper deck of a Routemaster bus?
18. NATIONAL GALLERY – estimate the size of da Vinci's *Virgin on the Rocks*. Do not touch it. What is the oldest picture in the gallery?

19. LEICESTER SQUARE – how many telephone booths are there in the square? What is showing at the Odeon this week?
20. QUEEN ELIZABETH II CONFERENCE CENTRE – when was it opened? Who by? Who designed it?
21. BRITISH MUSEUM – who is the curator? What are the Elgin Marbles now called? What do they depict? How many are there?
22. CENOTAPH – what inscription is written on it?
23. MONUMENT – what is the Monument a monument to? What is written on it?
24. From what point are measurements of distance from London made?
25. ROYAL SHAKESPEARE COMPANY – what play is next being performed by the RSC at the Pit? Who designed the lighting for the production?
26. TATE GALLERY – what is the most valuable exhibit in cash terms? What is the smallest item on public display?
27. WESTMINSTER PIER – what is the cost of a return trip to Greenwich?
28. CLEOPATRA'S NEEDLE – where did it come from? How tall do you estimate it to be?
29. SOUTH BANK – estimate the length of the pedestrian bridge from Embankment Station to the South Bank.
30. LAMBETH PALACE – what colour is the main door painted on the inside?
31. EMBANKMENT STATION – what did Embankment Station used to be called?
32. NATIONAL THEATRE – produce a programme of forthcoming plays at the three theatres.
33. FLEET STREET – what national papers are still printed in Fleet Street?
34. GRAYS INN ROAD – where and what is the Industrial Society?
35. OLD BAILEY – how many courts are there?
36. MORLEY COLLEGE – what evening classes do they offer in the third week?
37. ST PAUL'S CATHEDRAL – how many steps are there to the Whispering gallery? What is written on Wren's tomb?
38. NATIONAL GARDEN MUSEUM – two famous gardeners are buried here. What plant is named after them?
39. NATURAL HISTORY MUSEUM – who designed it? What is the entry fee?
40. What is the tallest building in London? How tall is it?

# Obits

**Summary**   Participants write their own obituaries.

**Objectives**   Self-disclosure.
Self-perception.

**Materials**   Whiteboard.
Pens.

**Timing**   15 minutes.

**Procedure**
1. Draw two large inverted "U" shapes on the board and invite participants to guess what they are. Acknowledge any wrong answers (even rude ones!) and explain that they actually are tombstones. One of them represents the tombstone they have made for themselves and one is a tombstone erected by others.
2. Invite participants to copy the two stones and write on them their epitaph for themselves and one for themselves as written by others.
3. Invite them to share with a partner.

**Commentary**   The sharing can be made an optional part of another self-disclosure activity.

**Variation**   Make it a newspaper obituary.

# Odd Objects

**Summary**
Description of objects using a restricted vocabulary.

**Objectives**
Written communication (specifically developing vocabulary, testing assumptions made in writing, use of thesaurus and letter-writing skills).

**Materials**
Newsprint.
A number of wrapped objects (such as a mascara, a teabag, nut-crackers, a pipe, a fan, a banana).
Marker pens.
Newsprint.
Lists of "forbidden words" that relate to the objects to be described.

**Timing**
40 minutes.

**Procedure**
1. Ask the group to divide itself into two. Move them into separate rooms and give each group an object.
2. Ask participants to write to the other group describing their object without saying what it is and without using any of the words on the list or any derivatives of them.
3. Swap the letters when completed and ask the groups to draw the object described.
4. Discuss the drawings in the group, and ask them to critique each other's letters.

**Commentary**
Objects must be easy to draw and of an everyday character. The list of forbidden words can be developed by adding the ones discovered by each group. A sample list for three of the objects suggested above is given below. Make sure that you include a reference to "any brand name". This is a good exercise for the end of a working day.

The title of the game is from a song by Laurie Anderson (Anderson 1984).

**Variations**
With a large group it is necessary to have three or four groups (all working in separate rooms) and then to swap the letters.

**Sample lists of forbidden words**

MASCARA – any brand name, mascara, cosmetic, eye, lash, lid, face, beauty, wand, bristle, hair, female, black, pupil.

TEA BAG – tea, bag, char, kettle, mug, cup, chimpanzee, perforation, saucer, lemon, sugar, milk, leaf, any brand name, any place where tea is made.

FAN – cool, air, breeze, hot, summer, jungle, tropical, Madam Butterfly, Japan, paper, face, hand, wave, wind.

# One A

**Summary**    Naming of words beginning with a set letter.

**Objectives**    Energizer.
Attention switching.

**Materials**    Ball.

**Timing**    Ten minutes.

**Procedure**    1.  Arrange the group in a circle with the trainer at the centre. Explain that they are to pass the ball round from person to person, starting now.
2.  Explain that you will clap your hands and then call out a letter of the alphabet. When you clap your hands a second time the person who last touched the ball is to call out three words beginning with that letter before the ball goes round the circle and comes back to him or her. Failure means taking the role in the middle.

**Variations**    1.  The number of words to be repeated can be increased with the agreement of the group. It can also be varied with the number of claps of the person in the centre.
2.  Rather than words which start with a letter, the target words could be those that rhyme with a set word, words with a set number of syllables, that end with a certain letter, that do not have a certain letter in them, that belong to a certain category (for example adverbs), etc.

# On the Other Hand

**Summary**    One person providing the non-verbal support to another's words.

**Objectives**    Non-verbal communication.
Assertiveness.

**Materials**    None.

**Timing**    30 minutes.

**Procedure**    1.  Introduce the concept of non-verbal communication and the way that the "words" can sometimes contradict the "music". Link this with assertiveness if relevant to the course. Divide the group into pairs labelled A and B. Explain that A will be the speaker on a set topic: B will provide the non-verbal communication. A will stand in front of B and clasp B round the waist, and B will put his or her arms in front as if they were A's.
2.  After ascertaining what clarification is needed, ask pairs what their topics are and allocate topics (suggestions below) if they lack them.
3.  After each turn, open a discussion on what alternatives might be appropriate.

**Commentary**  A couple of rounds may well suffice, in which case it best to ask for volunteers.

**Variation**    The As can be placed in pairs facing each other. Most of the examples below can accommodate this.

**Suggested topics**

- a President announcing his resignation.
- a store demonstrator selling an electric potato peeler.
- scientist announcing a vaccine for AIDS.

- person conducting the last movement of Beethoven's Ninth Symphony.
- someone flirting at an office Christmas party.
- reading a bedtime story to a child.
- a reporter on a battlefront.
- a politician being interviewed after a major victory.
- someone talking about shoes they have recently bought.
- a parent explaining the facts of life.
- the winner of a long-distance race being interviewed.

# Packtivity

**Summary**       Relay game involving packs of playing cards.

**Objectives**    Energizer
                  Attention switching.

**Materials**     Two used packs of playing cards.
                  Chairs.

**Timing**        Ten minutes.

**Procedure**
1. Ask participants to form themselves into two teams and ask each team to seat themselves in a row, side-by-side. The two teams should be facing each other.
2. Place a used pack of cards (new ones do not grip very well) beside the team member at one end each row. Explain that the object of the game is to pass all the cards from one end of the team to the other as quickly as possible. The first team member holds the cards in the hand furthest from the rest of the team. S/he then moves one card to their other hand, passes it to the first hand of the second team member, who passes it from one hand to the other, and then on to the third team member. The last person in the team then puts the cards into a second pile on the floor. No team member should have more than one card in each hand at one time. Demonstrate the movements.
3. Play the game, giving verbal encouragement to participants to work quickly, and reminding them encouragingly of what they should be doing.

**Variations**
1. An extended version of the game can be played by timing the teams and then setting a time trial for a second round.
2. More teams can be used for a large group.
3. Two packs of cards can circulate in different directions.
4. Team members can be blindfolded.
5. One of the most successful relay games (not using cards) on a residential course involves teams putting covers onto duvets and taking them off again.

# Picture Hunt

**Summary**      Group members act as a team to duplicate a series of photographs of places in their city.

**Objectives**   Team-building.
Leadership.

**Materials**    Loaded instamatic camera for each team.
Street maps showing the location of the training venue.
Sets of prepared photographs.

**Timing**       Variable, depending on tasks used (about one and a half hours for an eight person team with the same time for processing).

**Procedure**
1.  Ask participants to arrange themselves into teams of no more than eight people. It is preferable to have one group only, and this will be possible if the number of tasks is varied. If there are one or two over the eight then some group members can be asked to serve as observers. They can then be swapped over during the exercise.
2.  Explain that each group will be given a series of photographs and a camera. Their task is to reproduce the photographs. They will be awarded points on the basis of the accuracy of their pictures:

   10 points for a picture of the same object or place from any angle
   50 points for a similar picture.
   100 points for a picture that is impossible to distinguish from the original.

The decision of the trainer in scoring will be final.
Participants will be given no further guidance on how to carry out these tasks. Explain that there is a non-negotiable time limit of one and a half hours on the completion of the task.

3. Monitor the groups (one trainer to each group) as they go about their tasks.
4. Ask the groups to present their findings: then ask what they learned about themselves while carrying out the exercise. Focus first on how the task was allocated, which (if any) pictures were not attempted, and how the job was prioritized (for instance, priority given to accuracy of pictures as opposed to number). Demonstrate roles taken by group members (such as Leader, Critic, Developer, Pragmatist, Inventor). Then focus on the feelings that the exercise evoked and how much of themselves group members invested in the task. Discuss how what was learned can be applied back at work.

**Commentary** Try to keep the comments by the trainer before the exercise starts to a minimum.

The pictures should be of the building in which the course is taking place and the surrounding area. Try to disguise them by taking pictures through high windows, in the reflection of mirrors and windscreens, between your legs, etc., but do not include people or anything which would make the picture too hard to reproduce, or which would require participants to go to places where they would not be allowed on the grounds of safety. You could include the trainer in pictures and see if participants try to persuade you to assume the same position. This game is based on the same principles as **Naked City** (p. 98).

**Variations** 1. Time penalties can be imposed for questions asked of the trainer.
2. Competition can be made more or less important by the way that the groups are treated. It is even possible to state that the team that finishes first will be the winner.

# Pillow Talk

**Summary**       Meetings game allowing every person to have a say.

**Objectives**    Listening skills.
Decision making.
Assertiveness.

**Materials**     Pillow or other soft object.
Chairs (optional).

**Timing**        30 minutes.

**Procedure**     1.  Sit participants in a circle. The trainer introduces "the pillow". Participants can only speak when someone has passed them the pillow. They can indicate they want it by raising one finger. The person holding the pillow can pass it to anyone else, hold on to it or put it in the middle where anyone may pick it up.
2.  Demonstrate these possibilities with examples involving other participants. Ask whether clarification is needed.
3.  Give a topic (or refer to one that the group already knows that it has to discuss).
4.  Discuss how the exercise felt.

**Commentary**    Try to find a topic which is of relevance to members of the group. Although at first this seems to be a long winded way of running a discussion, everyone who speaks knows that they are being listened to. Not listening is also indicated in a demonstrative way.

**Variations**    1.  Participants *must* comment in some way when the pillow is passed to them.
2.  The pillow can also be used to represent the problem, and people are only allowed to speak when they are exercising ownership of it. This is a good way to introduce the concept of problem ownership (see Clinard 1985, and Egan 1986).

# Poetry in Motion

**Summary**    Relaxation exercise based on T'ai Chi.

**Objectives**    Stress management.

**Materials**    Sound source and music (ambient or New Age music such as that of Kitaro is suitable).

**Timing**    From 20 minutes.

**Procedure**

1. Explain that some relaxation methods aim to help you unwind (fantasies) and others alert you (Shiatsu). This third kind unites mental calm with physical movement. It is based on a Chinese practice of T'ai Chi, the principle of making physical movement a flowing one.
2. Distribute participants where they have room to move freely. Explain that you are going to suggest movements, but that they should go at a pace that seems right for them.
3. Turn on the background music. Then go through the movements slowly and with pauses:

   (i) Spread your feet about shoulder-width apart and parallel. Feel your breathing.
   (ii) Let your knees bend slightly. Allow your pelvis to tip forward. Feel the weight of your stomach come off your diaphragm. Feel your diaphragm and chest relax.
   (iii) Feel a weight, a centre of balance behind your navel. Feel the heaviness of it holding you in balance.
   (iv) Let your head float like a balloon. Roll it round in small circles until you find a comfortable position. Raise your face until you are looking almost level.
   (v) Feel your back gently tighten like the string of a kite between the balloon of your head and the anchor of your abdomen. Feel the rhythm of your breathing.
   (vi) Hold your tongue gently against the roof of your mouth.

      (vii)  Focus on your legs and on the gentle shifting balance from one leg to the other. Gently straighten the lighter leg. Very slowly make an *empty* step forward, heel first, keeping your weight on the bent leg until the straight one is flat on the earth again. Experiment moving forward and backward. Feel the energy moving through your body from one leg to the other, from one arm to the other. Feel the energy moving you. That sense of harmonious motion is one that you can have whenever you want.

    4.   Suggest that this is something that participants might wish to practice at home before work.

**Commentary**  Ensure that you are quite familiar with all the movements before you go through them with a class. When you have decided on a version of the exercise that you can use then the instructions can be turned into a handout.

**Variations**  Imagery can be used, and the movements made more subtle and complicated.

# Remote

**Summary**    Exercise in having control over others, or being controlled by taking the role of a robot.

**Objectives**    Negotiation.
Team-building.

**Materials**    A well-furnished room.

**Timing**    30 minutes.

**Procedure**

1. Ask participants to form pairs and label themselves A and B. Explain that A will be the controller and B will be the robot.
2. Controllers have their right arm raised from the elbow. Robots perform *any* task commanded by the controller. Seek clarification and then play the game for three minutes.
3. Explain that from now on robots should obey any controller who commands them.
4. Ask if participants want to reverse the roles (the robots will!). Then discuss participants' feelings about the exercise.

**Commentary**    It is interesting to ask at the end of the first round if the robots would mind missing the second round to do a different exercise. There will be great reluctance, which can be used to open the idea of natural justice.

The theme of personal responsibility under authority can also emerge from this activity. I have used the example of being told to pour a glass of water over someone's head and only being stopped at the last minute. If I had not been stopped and had then been accused (for example) of ruining an expensive perm I would have said "it wasn't my fault. S/he told me to do it", and I really felt that was the case (compare the Holocaust).

This game can also be used to explore the effect of single as opposed to multiple chains of command (on the manager and the managed), the effect of losing control over staff, sabotage, and revenge. It is also useful in team-building exercises, where the controller and controlled are of a different status in the team.

**Variation**     The robots are blindfolded and have to identify their controller by voice and touch.

# Research Rap

**Summary**    Exercise in giving presentations before a group.

**Objectives**    Presentational skills.
Team-building.

**Materials**    Any presentational materials asked for by the group (OHP, white-board, paper, etc.).
Research materials.

**Timing**    One hour.

**Procedure**
1. Invite participants to form groups and make a presentation on a course-related topic. Explain the two principles of effective presentation: the need to establish what are the learning points, and the need to consider what method of presentation is going to "grab" the audience. Refer to some of the techniques used by other groups in the past, and to some of the strategies that you have adopted with them.
2. Negotiate preparation time, and while groups are preparing float between groups, offering advice where necessary.
3. Carry out a series of presentations, reminding those acting as the audience of their responsibility to react appropriately and with enthusiasm.

**Commentary**    The quality of the product depends very much upon the quality of the research material that is made available to the groups. Groups will require different amounts of support and encouragement, and it is important to offer neither too much nor too little. Impress on them the fact that they are assuming responsibility for covering the teaching points of their topic. The other important variable is the guidance you give them on presentational method.

Anyone who has undertaken trainer training will have their own ideas on this, and there are many references such as Eitington (1989).

**Variation**    List topics and invite participants to "sign up" for what they want to do on a first-come-first-served basis, with a maximum for each group.

# Resents and Appreciates

**Summary**      Ventilation of feelings about the course.

**Objectives**   Assertiveness.
Self-disclosure.
Feedback (to trainer).
Validation.

**Materials**    None.

**Timing**       Ten minutes.

**Procedure**    1.  Invite participants to take it in turn to express a "resent" and
an "appreciate" about any aspect of what has happened that
day. It could be an aspect of the course content, or even something about what they did at lunch.
2.  Explain that this should take the form "I resented it when . . ."
and "I appreciated it when . . ." so as to focus on specific
events, focus on their own feelings, and not allocate blame to
other people. The option remains to "resent nothing" and "to
appreciate nothing", but participants should be discouraged
from saying nothing at all.
3.  If nobody volunteers start off yourself.

**Commentary** This is related to the assertion exercise **Goodies** (p. 71). It is a good
exercise to have at the end of each day of a long course.

**Variations**   1.  If assertiveness is a theme of the course then ask them to end
with "I appreciate myself for."
2.  Alternative phraseology can be "my good thing" and "my bad
thing".

# A Right Pickle

**Summary**    Game estimating the number of pickled onions in a jar.

**Objectives**    Team-building.
Decision making.

**Materials**    Large (catering size) jar of pickled onions which you have previously counted.
Flipchart and pens.
Calculator.

**Timing**    25 minutes.

**Procedure**
1. Present the group with a jar of pickled onions and ask partici-pants – from their position – to estimate how many there are in the jar. Take the estimates in and use them to calculate the average guess.
2. Ask the group members to guess again and calculate a second average.
3. Repeat this twice more, ending with an individual guess.
4. Reveal the actual number of pickled onions and ask the group to discuss how their guesses had changed. Were they closer than they had been before? Why? What had they taken into account?
5. At the end of the exercise, or at a suitable later point, pass round the jar for participants to eat a pickled onion.

**Commentary**    This is a simplification of the Delphi decision making method (named after the oracle of ancient Greece), which is outlined in Eitington (1989, pp. 170–72), who gives further references. When the procedure is used for decision making it is ideas and decisions which are being ranked rather than estimates. There is, however, an important team-building objective in the realization that a group can make better decisions when knowledge is shared among all its members.

**Variations**
1. Two groups can be run. One where the average is fed back

118

and one where it is not. Or one where false feedback or feedback taking into account only some of the estimates is given.

2. The object can be varied, but pickled onions are the right size for group members to have a good guess at, are edible, can be replenished from a supply, and will not decay between training events!

# Sharks

**Summary**     Energizer based on surviving in shark infested waters.

**Objectives**     Energizer.
Assertiveness

**Materials**     Large pieces of paper (at least A1).

**Timing**     Five minutes.

**Procedure**     1.   Place several large pieces of paper on the floor of a room where the chairs have been cleared to the edges.
2.   Explain that participants are to imagine that they are swimming in shark infested water. They are to swim round the islands represented by the pieces of paper. On the call "sharks" they are to make it to one of the islands.
3.   Progressively reduce the number of islands until there is only one left.

**Commentary**     Participants need encouragement through the game to stop swimming too close to the islands. What usually happens is that they pile onto the islands, grab onto each other and topple off. Depending on the level of processing, the trainer wishes to reach, assertiveness can be processed by considering who gives in and when. Suggesting that participants take their shoes off is a good way to stop them getting too rough.

# Shiatsu Shuffle

**Summary**      Energizing relaxation exercise.

**Objectives**   Energizer.
                 Stress management.

**Materials**    None.

**Timing**       About ten minutes.

**Procedure**    1. Explain that there are some forms of massage that calm people down and others that stimulate them for activity. This is one of the latter. It is based on the principle of Shiatsu or acupressure: that there are some points on the head, feet and hands that are directly connected to the rest of the body. Massage on these points is particularly effective. It can also do *no harm*. Ask that participants take their shoes and socks off and place themselves into a comfortable position.
                 2. Explain that the massage method uses the *middle fingers* of each hand or the *knuckles and thumbs*. The movements are *kneading, circular and pressing* and are firmer than they may be used to in massage.
                 3. *Foot*: start with the feet. Begin with the ankle bones, then the triangle between the ankle, heel and tendon, the bottom of the foot along the edge of the instep, the bottom of the foot along the base of the toes, then pull and twist the toes, move to the top of the foot in a raking movement from the toes up. Finally, slap the bottom of the foot all over.
                 4. *Hands*: pinch the finger ends, pull and twist fingers, knead cushion at base of fingers on inside, then palm and heel of hand, then the pad between thumb and first finger, the outside of the wrist below the knuckle, ending in a raking movement along back of fingers.
                 5. *Head*: start with forehead and work round eye socket, pinch bridge of nose, cheeks, under the nose, line of the jaw temples, following hairline to skull at back of head and back to temple. Pull ears and pinch ear lobes. Tap head all over with finger ends.

**Commentary** This should be energetically modelled by the trainer at all stages. The trainer must be thoroughly familiar with all of the movements involved. Further details of Shiatsu practices and the underlying principles (which can be taken to very high levels of complexity) are to be found in Maxwell-Hudson (1988).

# Sixty-Second Solos

**Summary**        Presentations exercise taking one minute.

**Objectives**     Presentational skills.
                   Team-building.

**Materials**      Circle of chairs.
                   Material as required by participants.
                   Flipchart and pens.

**Timing**         45 minutes or longer (timings based on a group of 12).

**Procedure**   1.  Offer to have participants make a presentation lasting one minute, where each participant will remember each of the presentations.
                2.  Ask for ideas, gripes, proposals for change or whatever, and put them on the board with the name of the proposer. Hold an auction where everyone has £1000, bidding starts at £5, and anyone with money left at the end gets a forfeit, which in fact isn't worth it. The forfeit is that anyone without a topic at the end is asked to choose their own, since the ones there obviously weren't worth that much to them.
                3.  Emphasize that each presentation will be followed by feedback from participants (with no response from the trainer) on what they learned from the presentation. The presenter has *sixty seconds* and must ensure that the learning points that s/he wants to hear do actually come out. Give some examples (such as "He/she's always on the phone", illustrated by the presenter dancing round another person lying on a picture of a telephone, collecting watches to demonstrate "I never have enough time" and 45 seconds of mumbling followed by loud lapel grabbing to demonstrate "You need to grab your audience".)
                4.  Offer to spend time with anyone having trouble developing their presentation. Allow ten minutes preparation time. Encourage participants to use physical means of presentation, and to use each other as accomplices or props as required.
                5.  Run the presentations in sequence quite quickly with the feedback session as in Stage 3. Allow the presenter to tickle mem-

ories with a word or two if the desired point doesn't come across. Test recall by displaying the sheet later in the course.

**Commentary** This is a good exercise in bringing about change in an organization. Senior management often realize they have allowed themselves to be blinded to some things.

# Speaking Statues

**Summary**     Exercise in descriptions without non-verbal communication.

**Objectives**  Non-verbal communication.

**Materials**   Two cards with "water going down a plughole" and "a spiral stair-case" written on them.

**Timing**      30 minutes.

**Procedure**   1. Form the participants into two groups. Give each group one of the cards.
                2. Tell each group that their task is to have one of the group members stand up in front of the other group and describe the thing on the card.
                3. The groups are to discuss how they will do this, and elect their speaker. The trainer then explains that they must keep their hands by their sides and not move.
                4. Go through the presentations and hold a discussion focusing on:

                   – What was difficult about the task?
                   – What would have been different about being able to move their hands?
                   – How it was like standing up in front of a group?
                   – How the group came to a decision as to how to carry out the talk?

**Variation**   The speaker can be asked to be blindfolded.

# Spokes-People

**Summary**    Representation of important people in one's life.

**Objectives**    Self-disclosure.
Team-building.

**Materials**    Whiteboard.
Newsprint.
Paper and pens.

**Timing**    20 minutes.

**Procedure**

1. Begin by explaining that everyone has important people in the wheel of their life, and these can be considered as spokes. Invite them to write down the names of the ten most important people in their lives.
2. Ask them to draw a diagram starting with an upright line which forms the radius for a circle with an arrowhead (see Figure 1).
3. Explain that this is to form the basis of a wheel to represent those people. The clockwise distance can represent the time in one's life and the length of the lines can represent the importance that the person had for you at that time. Draw an example on the whiteboard (along the lines of Figure 2).
4. Invite participants to form pairs, and discuss how the decisions were reached and how they came to be where they are, what they might want to change, what they need to make that change, and how the course might help.
5. If required, have a group discussion on what people have learned about themselves.

**Variations**

1. The dimensions used can be varied as necessary.
2. Participants can be asked to draw the diagram as they were five years ago, or as they would wish to be.
3. The people described can be chosen from those in the workplace in a team-building course. In this case the focus of the discussion might change.

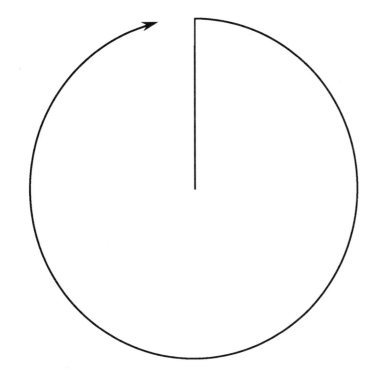

**Figure 1**

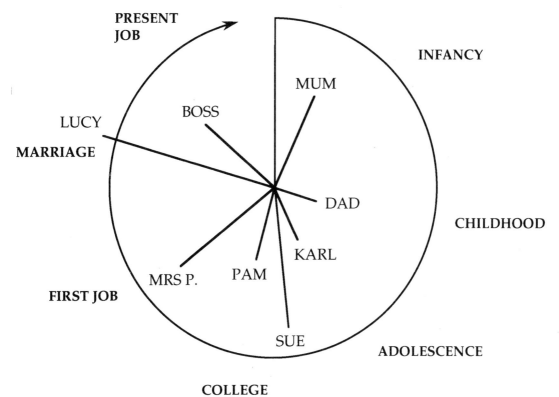

**Figure 2**

127

# STD

**Summary**     Observation testing energizer.

**Objectives**   Energizer.
Attention switching.
Non-verbal communication.

**Materials**    None.

**Timing**       Seven minutes.

**Procedure**    1. Ask group to line up in pairs facing each other and take a good look at each other for 60 seconds.
2. Ask pairs to face away from each other and change "three things about the way they look (for example, smile, close one eye, cross arms, untie shoelace, remove glasses, move a ring from one finger to another).
3. Have participants face each other again for 60 seconds and try to spot what has been changed.
4. If there is time, change partners and repeat.
5. Discuss which changes were noticed and which were not.

**Commentary** The title is an abbreviation for "Spot The Difference".

**Variation**    Have partners with their eyes closed for Stage 3 and find out by touch. This introduces a trust element.

# Stoned

**Summary**    A configuration of stones represents aspects of group function.

**Objectives**    Team-building.
Self-disclosure.

**Materials**    A large box of small stones that are different.

**Timing**    30 minutes.

**Procedure**    1.    Hand out stones, ask participants to choose one with which they can identify, and give five minutes for them to get to know it.
2.    Form participants in a circle and invite them to arrange their stones in a circle a foot in front of them. Ask them to move forward, looking at the circle of stones and see if their position is properly represented. Perhaps they want to be nearer some people's stones and further from others?
3.    When everyone is happy with their position, start a discussion of how people felt about where they were and how others moved relative to them. Ask if they can relate the stones to where they are in the group.
4.    Invite participants to keep their stones.

**Commentary**    The processing of this activity often takes much longer than the activity itself.

**Variation**    Play the game with one person moving all of the stones. In this case, first ask each person to introduce their stone to the rest of the group, pointing out its interesting features.

# Story Game

**Summary**     Inference game based on a passage of text.

**Objectives**  Listening skills.
Attributions.
Written communication.

**Materials.**  Prepared sheets.
Pens.

**Timing**      45 minutes.

**Procedure**   1.  Hand out the sheets and read out the instructions. Check whether anything needs clarifying. Explain that you will give participants five minutes to read the story and answer the questions.

2.  Ask participants to compare their answers in pairs for five minutes and try to reconcile differences. Afterwards ask them to consider

    (i)   Were there any surprises in the answers?
    (ii)  What assumptions might the story encourage you to make, and why?
    (iii) What are the implications for the way we communicate with each other?

3.  Go through the "correct" answers with the group. Emphasize that they are not being judges on the number that they get right, but examining why distortions were made.

4.  Discuss the number that participants got wrong. What kinds of inference were they making? What were they assuming? Do they ever do anything like that in real life? How factual was the material? Did it seem unambiguous? How much more likely are people to make wrong inferences in material about feelings and motivations?

**Commentary** Do not place too much stress on the "right" answers. They are only the means to a learning objective. The time limit may be used by participants as an excuse for wrong answers. If so, clarify whether they think they would have got all the answers right without the limit. How often in everyday life do they have to interpret within a time limit? The processing will be more specific where stereotyping and prejudice are the learning objectives – my own twist to a fairly classic training exercise. Loftus (1979) is a classic text on systematic distortions on recall by questioning.

**Variations**

1. Dispense with the time limit.
2. Use a different story or questions.
3. Read the story aloud.

# The Story Game

## The riddle publishing story

*Instructions*
Read the story and assume that everything stated in it is true. Read it carefully. Do not try to memorize the contents.

Read the numbered statements about the story (on the next page) and decide whether each one is true, false or cannot be decided on the basis of the story. Circle the "T" if you are sure the statement is true; circle the "F" if you think the statement is false; circle the "?" if you cannot decide on the basis of the information given. If you feel doubtful about any part of a statement, then circle the question mark.

Please take the statements in turn – do not go back later to change any of the answers you have made. Also, do not re-read any of the statements overleaf after you have answered them. Such altering or re-reading will distort the test.

Thank You.

## The story
Pat Bolton, Managing Director of Riddle Publishing, received a telephone call from the Nottingham District Manager, Peter Macdonald. During the call Bolton mentioned the possibility of Macdonald resiting the East Midlands office in a converted warehouse. Macdonald explained that a recent architecture graduate named Madood could design the conversion, and Bolton agreed that Madood should be interviewed.

# Statements about the Story

1. Riddle Publishing is a limited company.

          T          F          ?

2. Riddle Publishing is run by a man named Pat Bolton.

          T          F          ?

3. Peter Macdonald telephoned Pat Bolton.

          T          F          ?

4. Macdonald and Bolton were in different towns.

          T          F          ?

5. Macdonald and Bolton discussed resiting the Nottingham office.

          T          F          ?

6. Bolton initiated the conversation about re-siting of the East Midlands regional Office.

          T          F          ?

7. The story does not state whether Madood is a qualified architect.

          T          F          ?

8. In their conversation Bolton and Macdonald discussed contracting a young architect called Madood.

          T          F          ?

9. Macdonald did not tell Bolton anything he had heard about Madood.

          T          F          ?

10. Bolton promised to interview Madood.

          T          F          ?

11. The gist of the story is that one man calls another to recommend a third man.

          T          F          ?

12. Bolton and Macdonald discussed a recent college graduate named Madood.

T         F         ?

13. The story does not state clearly whether Bolton had reservations about Madood's suitability as an architect.

T         F         ?

14. Pat Bolton is a manager with Riddle Publishing.

T         F         ?

# Statements about the Story with Correct Answers

1. Riddle Publishing is a limited company.
   Unknown – it could be a partnership.
2. Riddle Publishing is run by a man named Pat Bolton.
   Unknown – Pat Bolton could be a woman.
3. Peter Macdonald telephoned Pat Bolton.
   True.
4. Macdonald and Bolton were in different towns.
   Unknown – they could have been using car phones.
5. Macdonald and Bolton discussed resiting the Nottingham Office.
   Unknown – the office might not have been in Nottingham.
6. Bolton initiated the conversation about resiting the East Midlands Regional Office.
   Unknown.
7. The story does not state whether Madood is a qualified architect.
   False.
8. In their conversation Bolton and Macdonald discussed contracting a young architect graduate called Madood.
   Unknown – Madood could have been a mature student.
9. Macdonald did not tell Bolton anything he had heard about Madood.
   False.
10. Bolton promised to interview Madood.
    Unknown – it is not clear who would do the interviewing.
11. The gist of the story is that one man calls another to recommend a third man.
    Unknown – Madood and Bolton could have been women.
12. Bolton and Macdonald discussed a recent college graduate named Madood.
    False – Madood might not have been a college graduate.
13. The story does not state clearly whether Bolton had reservations about Madood's suitability as an architect.
    True.
14. Pat Bolton is a manager with Riddle Publishing,
    True.

# Subculture

**Summary**     Comparison of perceptions of the culture of a group.

**Objectives**     Team-building.

**Materials**     Copies of the Subculture worksheet (5 per person).

**Timing**     One hour.

**Procedure**     1.  Hand out copies of the worksheet and ask participants to complete them individually in about ten minutes.
2.  Ask participants to find a partner and compare their sheets. Using a further sheet, see if they can find a middle ground which satisfies them both. Explain that it does not matter if they do not.
3.  Have the pairs work with other pairs progressively until the whole group has been brought together.
4.  Open a discussion on whether there is a consensus that a group culture does exist which applies in some way to all the people present. What have people learned about the different way that their organization is perceived by its members? What have they learned about their own perceptions? Have those perceptions changed?

**Commentary**     This is a projective exploration of culture which attempts to tap participants' own models of their organization. For an examination of more theoretical approaches see Handy (1985, chapter 7).

**Variation**     Allow an anonymous exchange of completed worksheets by dumping them in the centre and redistributing before going onto Stage 2 of the game. This is a low-risk version of the game involving less self-disclosure.

# Subculture Worksheet

Complete the following statements. Think of at least three different endings to each statement:

In my organization you can . . .

In my organization you cannot . . .

In my organization you must . . .

In my organization you must not . . .

My organization sees itself as looking like a . . .

To succeed in my organization you have to . . .

The failures in my organization are the people who . . .

The motto of my organization would be . . .

The epitaph of my organization would be . . .

# Telling It

**Summary**   In pairs, participants disclose information about themselves in a structured way.

**Objectives**   Self-disclosure.
Team-building.

**Materials**   Prepared question cards (see p. 140).

**Timing**   90 minutes.

**Procedure**
1. Invite members to form pairs and allocate themselves as A and B. Distribute sets of questions on cards (selected from those below).
2. Invite pairs to work through the questions. They can tackle the questions in any order they like. It does not matter if they do not answer all (or even any) of the questions. Stress that answers will not have to be discussed outside of the pair.
3. Participants are only allowed to ask questions that

    (a) they are prepared to answer themselves, and
    (b) their partner is prepared to answer.

    For example, A would first decide whether s/he is prepared to answer question 1, and if so ask "are you prepared to answer question 1?" If B says "yes" then they can discuss their answers.
4. Allow a set time (say 15 minutes) to discuss the questions. Then ask participants to find a new partner, repeat again.
5. In the main group share feelings about the exercise, and if it can be done non-threateningly, ascertain the levels of self-disclosure (though not what was disclosed). Process how they decided which questions to answer. Examine the implications for the group in terms of trust and self-disclosure.

**Commentary**   The same list of questions can be used in **True Stories** (p. 144).

**Variations**   If the game is being used for exploring personal needs (for example, for team-building) then the second set of questions (p. 141) can be used. If it is being used for specific team-building purposes, then the third set of questions (p. 142) will be more appropriate. In this case, point to the two general closing questions and give a warning of the end of the turn so that pairs have time to consider those questions. It will be useful if there is enough trust in the group to disclose some of the findings of the group.

# List of General Self-disclosure Questions

1. What are you best at?
2. What do you most like about me?
3. If you won the pools what would you spend the money on?
4. What is the most cruel thing you have ever done to an animal?
5. What political party did you last vote for?
6. Who did you have a crush on when you were a teenager?
7. What colour underclothes are you wearing?
8. When was the last time you cried?
9. When did you last take something that did not belong to you?
10. What do you least like about me?
11. At what age do you think you will die?
12. What was your happiest moment?
13. What would you find a perfect evening?
14. Where would you most like to be right now?
15. What scares you most of all?
16. What was your nickname at school?
17. What is your favourite soap opera?
18. Whom have you ever wished was dead?
19. If there were a ten-minute warning for the end of the world what would you do?
20. What do you most like about yourself?
21. What makes you laugh the most?
22. If you could be anyone who would you like to be?
23. What would you most like to be able to do that you now can't?
24. What would you most like to change about yourself as you are now?
25. What would you most like me to say to you right now?
26. Who on this course do you find most attractive sexually?
27. How did you last break the law?
28. What are you most proud of having achieved in your life?
29. What is the most embarrassing thing that ever happened to you?
30. When in your life did you feel most sad?

BEFORE CLOSING THE ACTIVITY ANSWER THE FOLLOWING
    QUESTIONS
  1. How can we better help each other at work?
  2. How else can we jointly improve the effectiveness of our team?

140

# List of needs questions

*DO YOU HAVE A NEED FOR:*

solitude
company
relaxation
excitement
taking risks
reassurance
looking good
feeling fit
being healthy
being a leader
completing tasks on my own

giving affection
receiving affection
keeping my feelings to myself
being honest
being respected
having expertize
being part of a team
being asked to take part
being intelligent
being taken for granted

# List of Team-building Self-disclosure Questions

1. How happy are you in your present job?
2. How effective are you in your present job?
3. How efficient are you in your present job?
4. What do you see as the next step in the development of your career?
5. What are your main strengths at work?
6. What prevents you from using your strengths at work?
7. In what ways can I help you to make the most of your strengths at work?
8. What weaknesses prevent you from achieving what you might at work?
9. In what ways can I help you to overcome the effects of your weaknesses at work?
10. What do you wish had never happened in our [team*]?
11. What would you most like to happen in our [team*]?
12. What are the main achievements you are looking for in your work right now?
13. What do you think should be the goals of our [team*]?
14. What do you think prevents the [team*] from achieving its goals?
15. How would you characterize the leadership of our [team*]?
16. How do you perceive me?
17. How do you think I perceive you?
18. What was your impression of me when we first met?
19. How has your impression of me altered since we first met?
20. Are you enjoying this activity?
21. What barriers do you see to your own self-development?
22. What barriers do you see to your own advancement?
23. To whom are you closest in our [team*]?
24. From whom are you most distant in our [team*]?
25. How do you respond to pressure?
26. How committed are you to our [team*]?
27. What is your main contribution to our [team*]?
28. How do you feel about the feedback that you receive from our [team*]?
29. What things about me puzzle you?
30. How do you think our [team*] is seen by the rest of the organization?

*where necessary, replace with the appropriate word to describe the working group.

# Transporters

**Summary**     Exercise finding metaphors for an organization.

**Objectives**    Team-building.
Creativity.

**Materials**     Newsprint.
Pens.

**Timing**     25 minutes.

**Procedure**
1. Ask individuals to close their eyes, imagine what kind of vehicle their organization is and write it on newsprint.
2. Ask them to consider some questions about this vehicle. How many drivers does it have? How fast does it move? How does it tackle terrain? What fuel does it operate on? Ask them to write down their ideas.
3. Invite them individually or as a group to devise the ideal vehicle, taking into account whether it has a co-driver, how it communicates, its speed limit, and so forth.

**Commentary**  Metaphors and similes are a good way of making people think creatively about problems that they face (see Adams 1974, 1986).

**Variations**    This exercise can be carried out with animals or plays or novels or soap operas.

# True Stories

**Summary**   Participants answer questions about their feelings and beliefs.

**Objectives**   Introductions.
Self-disclosure.

**Materials**   Prepared cards (see p. 140).

**Timing**   15 minutes.

**Procedure**
1. Form the group into a circle and place cards face down in the middle of the group.
2. Explain that each card has a question on the other side, and invite them to take a card and answer as truthfully as they can the question on it. Suggest that if they do not feel able to answer the question they may trade it in for another.
3. Allow the answers to provoke discussion in a way that is non-threatening.

**Commentary**   The title comes from the David Byrne film. The same list of questions is used as in the exercise **Telling It** (p. 138).

# Two-Minute Talks

**Summary**  Presentational skills exercise.

**Objectives**  Presentational skills.
Team-building.

**Materials**  Any presentational materials asked for by group (OHP, whiteboard, paper, etc.).
Research materials.

**Timing**  20 minutes.

**Procedure**
1. List a series of topics on the whiteboard and invite participants to "sign up" for what they want to present a "two minute talk" on, do on a first-come-first-served basis, with a maximum for each group.
2. Explain that research material will be provided, and that they need not be afraid of standing up in front of the rest of the group as the others will be doing it too.
3. After ten minutes' preparation time (offering guidance where necessary), go through the presentations.

**Commentary**  The quality of the product depends very much upon the quality of the research material that is made available to the groups. Groups will require different amounts of support and encouragement, and it is important to offer neither too much nor too little. Emphasize that presentational skills are not being assessed. The general principles of **Research Rap** (p. 116) can be followed, but here there is much less emphasis on presentational skills. The objective is rather to make the essential points as concisely as possible.

# Validation Posters

**Summary**      Mutual validation of participants' contributions.

**Objective**    Validation.

**Materials**    Large pages of good quality paper (like flipchart paper).
Different coloured pen for each participant.

**Timing**       30 minutes.

**Procedure**
1. Introduce this as an end of course exercise. Hand out paper and ask each participant to write his/her name and briefly decorate it however they wish on a sheet of newsprint.
2. Put the sheets up round the room and invite participants to write "one positive statement" on each person's sheet.
3. Allow participants to retain their sheets.

**Variations**   The Trainer may participate or not as appropriate. If there are two trainers, then they should make genuine comments on each other's sheets as they will be seen by others.

# What are *You* Doing?

**Summary**  Turn-taking miming energizer.

**Objectives**  Energizer.
Attention switching.

**Materials**  None.

**Timing**  Ten minutes.

**Procedure**
1. Ask participants to form a circle facing inwards. Explain (and demonstrate) that the starter will mime an activity (such as ironing a shirt), and that the person next to them in the agreed direction will say (for example) "Andy, what are you doing?" The starter can reply with anything they like (such as "I'm cutting my toe nails"), and the second person will have to act out this new activity. The third person then asks what *they* are doing, and so on until the circle is completed.
2. Illustrate with examples. Some are given below.
3. When the activity has gone full circle then, if you have time, reverse it.

**Commentary**  This activity should be kept moving with a high level of energy. Modelling by the trainer is important. This is a very effective and popular energizer. Be warned – one inevitable mime is "picking my nose!"

## Examples of activity

Rock climbing.
Brushing my teeth.
Picking my nose.
Swimming.
Driving home.
The dusting.
Swatting a fly.
Making shortcrust pastry.
Assembling a deckchair.

# What would You Do?

**Summary**     Participants consider what social skills they would exercise in
            different problematical situations.

**Objectives**   Assertiveness.
            Self-disclosure.

**Materials**    Prepared cards (more than one per person).

**Timing**       40 minutes.

**Procedure**    1.  Form participants into a circle and give a card to each person,
                    face down. Explain that they have the option to return their
                    card and take another one if they wish.
                2.  Ask participants to read out the situation outlined on their card
                    and to suggest how they might deal with it. The group can
                    seek clarification.
                3.  Allow each participant to take a turn.
                4.  In processing, pay attention to the "it depends" replies. What
                    do they show about the concerns of the person making that
                    qualification. What other "it depends" qualifications might
                    other participants make?

**Variations**   1.  The situations can be elicited from the participants at an earlier
                    stage in the training session. On a teamwork course you can
                    select situations that relate directly to the function of the team.
                2.  At Stage 2, invite others to guess the participant's response
                    before they give it.

# Situations For Cards

You are accused of stealing money by someone in authority but you know you did not do it.

You suspect that a patient on your ward is having an affair with one of the nurses.

You see two young men beating up a police officer.

You see two police officers beating up a young man.

You are offered an expensive coat at a ridiculous price by a friend and you suspect that it may be stolen.

You are returning to your car on the top floor of a multi-storey car park late at night. There is no one else about and you see someone lurking in the shadows.

Your brother or sister discloses him or her self as homosexual.

You cut through a public park late at night to get home and are stopped by the park police. You know that you have had a couple of drinks.

You see someone shoplifting in a store.

You notice your next door neighbour's child frequently leaves home for school bruised and tearful.

You suspect your boss of having a drug problem.

Sitting in a pub in a strange town you are approached by a female prostitute.

You see a tramp lying in a busy street who could be ill or drunk and is being ignored by other people.

Your house is on fire. You have time to save only two items.

You witnessed an exchange in the car park at work that implies that someone of a higher grade than you but in a different part of the organization is taking bribes.

A friend owes you his or her half of an expensive meal you had together. Repayment has been promised for over a week ago. Your friend seems to be avoiding you.

Someone you know at work, but not a close friend, confides that they are HIV positive.

# Word Link

**Summary**   Energizer in which participants link words by their first and last letters.

**Objectives**   Energizer.
Attention switcher.
Listening skills.

**Materials**   None.

**Timing**   Ten minutes.

**Procedure**
1. Form participants into a circle. Explain that you will ask them in turn to say the name of a food. The *first* letter of each word should be the *last* letter of the previous word. "Word" can be a linked pair of words (such as "Christmas cake").
2. If someone is struck then others can drop hints. (like for "y" – "part of an egg").

**Variations**   Use place names, actors, sports personalities, names of plants or animals. Words can be restricted to ones related to topics covered on the course.

# References

Adams, James L. (1974) *Conceptual Blockbusting, A Guide to Better Ideas*, Penguin.

Adams, James L. (1986) *The Care and Feeding of Ideas*, Penguin.

Anastasi, Anne (1979) *Fields of Applied Psychology*, McGraw-Hill.

Anderson, Laurie (1984) *United States*, Harper and Row.

Bartlett, F. C. (1932) *Remembering, A Study in experimental and social psychology*, Cambridge University Press.

Belbin, R. M. (1981) *Management Teams*, Heinemann.

Benson, Jarlath (1987) *Working more creatively with groups*, Tavistock, London.

Beresford-Cooke, Carole (1984) *The Book of Massage*, Ebury Press.

Bryson, Bill (1990) *Dictionary of Troublesome Words (2nd edition)*, Penguin.

Buchler, I. B. and Nutini, H. G. (1969) *Game theory in the behavioural sciences*, University of Pittsburgh Press.

Clark, Neil and Fraser, Tony (1987) *The Gestalt Approach, an introduction for managers and trainers*, Roffey Park, Horsham.

Clark, N., Phillips, K. and Barker, D. (1984) *Unfinished Business*, Gower.

Clinard, Helen (1985) *Winning ways to succeed with people*, Gulf.

Dainow, Sheila and Bailey, Caroline (1988) *Developing Skills With People*, Wiley.

Egan, Gerard (1986) *The Skilled Helper*, Brooks/Cole.

Eitington, J. E. (1989) *The Winning Trainer*, Gulf.

Freud, A. (1936) *The Ego and the Mechanisms of Defence*, Hogarth Press.

Hampden-Turner, Charles (1981) *Maps of the Mind*, Mitchell Beazley.

Handy, Charles B. (1985) *Understanding Organisations (third edition)*, Penguin.

Hargie, Owen (1986) *Handbook of Communication Studies*, Routledge.

Hopkins, J. (1981) "Seeing yourself as others see you" *Social Work Today*, 12, 25: 10–13.

Institute of Personnel Management (1984) *Continuous Development: People at Work*.

Kakabadse, Andrew, Ludlow, Ron and Vinnicombe, Susan (1987) *Working in Organisations*, Gower, pp. 333–35.

Laird, Dugan (1985) *Approaches to Training and Development*, Addison Wesley.

Lloyd, Peter and Mayes, Andrew (1984) *Introduction to Psychology: An Integrated Approach*, Fontana.

Loftus, E. F. (1979) *Eyewitness testimony*, Harvard University Press.

Margerison, Charles and McCann, Dick (1990), *Team Management*, Mercury.

Maxwell-Hudson, Clare (1988) *The Complete Book of Massage*, Dorling Kindersley.

Meek, R. L. (1974) *Figuring Out Society*, Fontana.

Noon, James (1985) *"A " Time*, Chapman and Hall.

Pfeiffer, J. W. (1973) "Risk Taking", in Pfeiffer, J. W. and Jones, J. E., *The 1973 Annual Handbook for Group Facilitators*, University Associates, pp. 124–26.

Pfeiffer, J. W. and Jones, J. E. (1972) "Openness, collusion and feedback", in Pfeiffer, J. W. and Jones, J. E., *The 1972 Annual Handbook for Group Facilitators*, University Associates, pp. 197–201.

Rackham, N. (1977) *Behaviour Analysis in Training*, McGraw-Hill.

Rakos, Richard R. (1986) "Asserting and confronting", in Hargie, O., *Handbook of Communication Studies*, Routledge.

Ribeaux, Peter and Poppleton, Stephen (1978) *Psychology and Work*, Macmillan.

Stammers, Robert and Patrick, John (1975) *Psychology of Training*, Methuen.

Swenson, C. H. (1973) *Introduction to Interpersonal Relations*, Scott Foresman.

Turing, Alan (1950) "Computing machinery and intelligence", *Mind*, vol. LIX, No. 236.

# Consolidated index of games by objectives

| Objective | Title of game | Volume/Page | | Timing (minutes) |
|---|---|---|---|---|
| | What'll be my Line | 1 | 129 | 20 |
| | Word Search | 1 | 138 | 60 |
| **Creativity** | | | | |
| | Archaeological Digs | 2 | 13 | 30 |
| | Charoodles | 1 | 51 | 15 |
| | Class of their Own | 2 | 27 | 45 |
| | If Eggs Could Fly | 2 | 79 | 70 |
| | Pickpockets | 1 | 103 | 45 |
| | Problems without Words | 1 | 106 | 35 |
| | Re-inventing the Wheel | 1 | 107 | 45 |
| | Rules of the Game | 1 | 111 | 70 |
| **Decision making** | | | | |
| | Consensus | 1 | 55 | 60 |
| | Game Game | 2 | 63 | 45 |
| | Missing Link | 2 | 94 | 20 |
| | One Pound Auction | 1 | 99 | 15 |
| | Right Pickle | 2 | 118 | 25 |
| **Energizer** | | | | |
| | Antimastermind | 2 | 11 | 10 |
| | Archaeological Digs | 2 | 13 | 30 |
| | Body Hello | 1 | 44 | 10 |
| | Can I Come to the Party? | 2 | 23 | 10 |
| | Chain Whispers | 2 | 25 | 10 |
| | Charoodles | 1 | 51 | 15 |
| | Circular Reactions | 1 | 53 | 10 |
| | Continuum | 2 | 34 | 15 |
| | Convoy | 1 | 57 | 5 |
| | Exotic Fruits | 1 | 61 | 5 |
| | Fangs | 1 | 64 | 10 |
| | Fruit Relay | 1 | 70 | 10 |
| | Fruit Salad | 2 | 62 | 5 |
| | Go-Go | 2 | 70 | 10 |
| | Interviews | 1 | 79 | 40 |
| | Invisible Tug-of-War | 1 | 80 | 10 |
| | Knotty Problems | 1 | 82 | 10 |
| | Learnabout | 2 | 89 | 10 |
| | Lost for Words | 2 | 93 | 30 |
| | Mornington Crescent | 1 | 93 | 10 |
| | Name Plate Shuffle | 1 | 96 | 15 |
| | Number Crunches | 1 | 97 | 20 |
| | One-A | 2 | 105 | 10 |
| | On Your Face | 1 | 101 | 20 |
| | Pactivity | 2 | 108 | 10 |
| | Rude Aerobics | 1 | 110 | 10 |

| Objective | Title of game | Volume/Page | | Timing (minutes) |
| --- | --- | --- | --- | --- |
| | Knots | 2 | 88 | 15 |
| | Mirrors | 1 | 92 | 5 |
| | Who's Who | 1 | 134 | 15 |
| **Validation** | | | | |
| | Grouptalk | 2 | 74 | 20 |
| | Just a Minute | 1 | 81 | 30 |
| | Resents and Appreciates | 2 | 117 | 10 |
| | Sixty-second Solos | 2 | 123 | 45 |
| | Truth Option | 1 | 123 | 10 |
| | Validation Posters | 2 | 146 | 30 |
| **Verbal communication** | | | | |
| | A Gender Setting | 2 | 7 | 30 |
| | Amnesia | 1 | 34 | 15 |
| | Antimastermind | 2 | 11 | 10 |
| **Written communication** | | | | |
| | Antimastermind | 2 | 11 | 10 |
| | Bit Parts of Speech | 1 | 43 | 15 |
| | Fleet Street Fog | 2 | 59 | 25 |
| | Martians | 1 | 89 | 20 |
| | Odd Objects | 2 | 103 | 40 |
| | RSVP | 1 | 109 | 15 |
| | Word Search | 1 | 138 | 60 |